Your Confession

Your. Confession: Using the New Ritual

Leonard Foley, O.F.M.

Nihil Obstat:
   Rev. Hilarion Kistner, O.F.M.
   Rev. John J. Jennings

Imprimi Potest:
   Rev. Roger Huser, O.F.M.
   Provincial

Imprimatur:
   +Joseph L. Bernardin
   Archbishop of Cincinnati
   October 30, 1974

Cover design and photographs by Michael Reynolds

SBN-0-912228-17-2

Contents

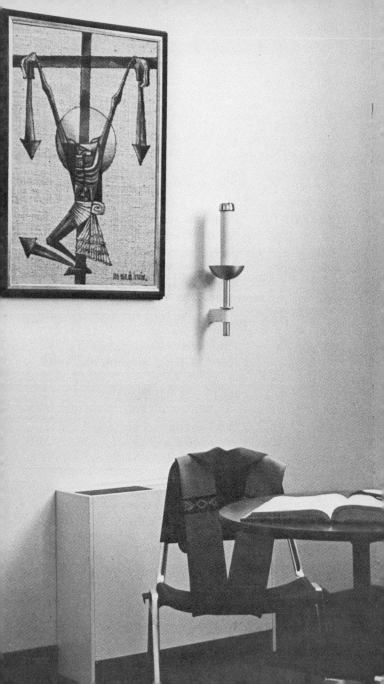

Chapter I

Problems
and Possibilities:
An Overview

The new ritual for confession attempts to carry out the mandate of Vatican II: "The rite and formulas for the sacrament of penance are to be revised so that they give more luminous expression to both the nature and effect of the sacrament" (Constitution on the Sacred Liturgy, No. 72).

Will it reawaken our badly damaged interest in the sacrament and bring back the great number of Catholics who now come to the sacrament rarely, if at all?

A reading of the lengthy introduction and the actual new rite may leave one with mixed feelings. There is nothing startlingly new. Individual confession puts a new stress on Scripture (though it can be minimally used), and there is a somewhat greater participation of the penitent in the prayers. The second mode of confession is already familiar to many as a "communal penance service" with individual confession and absolution. The third mode recognizes other occasions besides danger of death when general absolution may be given without individual confession (which is still to be made later in the case of mortal sinfulness). General absolution may also be given according to the new ritual when there is a "serious necessity, that is, when there are not enough priests on hand to hear individual confessions within a suitable time, so that penitents would be forced, without their fault, to be without the grace of the sacrament or would be kept from Holy Communion for a long time."

The fourth chapter of the ritual contains a plentiful supply of alternative Scripture texts and prayers. Appendices contain examples of non-sacramental penance services, with special celebrations for Lent and Advent. There are examples of penance services for children who have not yet made their first confession, for young people, for the sick. Lastly there is an outline for use in the examination of conscience "to be completed and adapted according to local customs and the differing situation of penitents."

Those who expected something radically new or different will be disappointed. Yet the revision is significant because there are new and positive emphases which, *if they become part of our understanding and experience,* will restore this sacrament to its rightful place in the life of the church. Some of these emphases are new (or renewed): the notion of *reconciliation,* and the *social nature* of sin and grace. Others are perennial: the mercy of God, our union with the death and rising of Christ, the outpouring of the Spirit, the living and visible community of the

Body of Christ called church, the need for depth and interiorization of faith.

Problems

What, then, are the problem areas that have to be dealt with before the new ritual can become a fitting expression of sacramental reconciliation? From many friendly wranglings during adult religious education meetings, I can identify four principal ones.

1. Trivialization, missing the real point. The way some of us have been "going" to confession and the way some of us priests have been "administering" the sacrament gave the impression, at least, that we were dealing with petty and trifling fluff. No doubt for most people this kind of confessing was a symbol of their real sinfulness — but the symbol could be terribly diluted. If Pete Nitney's basic sinfulness is a domineering personality, then "I missed my morning prayers" is scarcely a heartfelt expression of the *real evil* in his life. If Mrs. Sharptooth's basic and real sinfulness is a closed and bitter attitude toward her husband, she is scarcely on target when she goes on and on about distractions in prayer, gossip and coming late to Sunday Mass, never mentioning the coldness and rejection of her husband. And if what Smartaleck should really do is apologize to his parents for his insolence, three Hail Mary's are hardly a meaningful penance.

2. Loss of fear of mortal sinfulness. After verging towards one extreme, we seem to have moved toward another. Instead of worrying about "everything" being a mortal sin, we have perhaps come to the conclusion that "nothing" is a mortal sin.

It is a healthy development to realize that mortal sinfulness is a matter of ongoing and pervasive attitude — an across-the-board "fundamental option." It is really a "serious matter." We are blessed to be rid of the Jansenist heresy that implied, if it didn't come right out and say so, that almost no one could remain out of mortal sin very long and would therefore have to confess before practically every Communion. Now that this unwholesome fear has been largely dissipated, however, we may be finding ourselves without even a healthy fear or realistic sense of sin. With a questionable motive gone, do we find ourselves without any motive at all?

3. *The Catholic heresy of "only a venial sin."* Some Catholics frankly admit today that they just don't think that "venial" sins are important — certainly not worth going to confession for. It's like being so relieved that I don't have cancer, real or imagined (No. 2, above) that I am not concerned at all about persistent coughing or headaches, infected teeth or a continual fever.

It is one thing to get rid of the trivial non-sins and nonsense of the grocery list: I *forgot* my morning prayers; I ate meat on Friday (but I thought it was Thursday); I missed Mass but I was sick; I had bad thoughts but I tried to get rid of them; I want to include all doubtful sins against, etc. But it's an entirely different matter to consider the real infections of our life. If mortal sinfulness is an ongoing attitude, so is venial sinfulness a real infection in our Christian life. Our greatest problem may be to face

4

these continuing, conscious and freely adopted attitudes that are, simply, *evil*: selfishness, prejudice, vindictiveness, neglect, stubbornness, carelessness, etc.

An excellent article in *St. Anthony Messenger* (May, 1973), "A New Look at Mortal Sin," described the modern theologians' emphasis on the fact that mortal sinfulness (like faith) represents precisely the same attitude carried to its conclusion: a fundamental attitude that underlies my whole life. In the same way, venial sinfulness, if it is indeed real sinfulness, is serious — an infection, a weakness, a current of poison affecting my life all the time.

But it may just be simply human nature to take anything but death lightly. A new ritual alone will not change our attitude.

4. Loss of self-discipline. In an air-conditioned and comfort-oriented society, many of us have found it easy to skip some of the more demanding practices of our Catholic past: giving up candy or cigarettes during Lent, attending other services than Sunday Mass, avoiding the movies and books we thought unbecoming to a Christian spirit, saying morning and evening and meal prayers. Regular "devotional" confession seems to be another casualty of affluence.

Some will argue that it takes an enormous amount of self-discipline just to get through one day in this pressure-cooker society we have created. Penance, they say, is simply adapting to all the tensions that possess our lives. No doubt there is truth in this. But it does seem incongruous, doesn't it, that the disciplinary and "self-mortifying" aspect of religion seems to be most vividly exemplified in the Miami

Dolphins' training camp and George Foreman's gymnasium?

Will the New Ritual
Transform the Sacrament?

A ritual calls for a set of external actions. It can be as meaningful as "Good morning!" and as meaningless as — "Good morning." Ritual is like language: it is as essential as our skin and as open to use or abuse as our TV set. Ritual depends on the meaning people give it. If we don't *mean* Eucharist, baptism, reconciliation, our actions are obviously, meaning*less*. The technical theological statement that the sacraments "work" of themselves does not mean they can be isolated "out there" like money in the bank.

The new ritual won't work miracles. It won't be enough for us to start parroting phrases like "celebration of the mercy of God" and "reconciliation with the Body of Christ." The meaning of the beautiful words will have to be *interiorized*.

When a team is in trouble (and we're in trouble as far as confession is concerned), a return to fundamentals can sometimes get them back on the track. Perhaps a consideration of four basic Christian needs may ready us for the new ritual.

1. The need to experience community. There's no use talking about confession if people are not convinced that they need *church,* still less that they *are* church. And they won't believe they *are* church unless they experience being a community. Our problem is not how to get teenagers to Sunday Mass,

6

but to have something alive and personal when they get there.

Some Catholics are now saying what we used to blame those bad Protestants for: "Why not go straight to God? Why go to a priest?" The first question eliminates the church; the second then becomes irrelevant.

The phenomenon of prayer groups and charismatic meetings indicates an answer that is coming from the grass roots. We need to have the visible support and welcome of other persons. We need community. Better, we need to *experience community,* a sense of belonging to a definite group which welcomes us and to which we owe similar concern and responsibility.

It shouldn't be necessary to ask, but isn't that what the church is supposed to be? It is not some impersonal organization like the U.S. government or General Motors — individual tax checks and individual dividends passing through a cold and bloodless computer system. The church is that visible group of people which makes the love of Christ visible to each other and to the world. Only if I experience belonging to such a group — giving and receiving, feeling both the love of others and the desire to return it — will I realize that my sins are not just between God and me but that they involve my brothers and sisters also — by betrayal, bad example, weakening of spirit. I will see no need to "celebrate" any "reconciliation" if I feel no joy in being with them in the first place, and no sense of hurting them in the second place. So, fundamentally, we will have to deepen our idea of "church." And the only way we will do this is by *experiencing* it. You can't learn to swim by reading a book.

2. The need for leadership. Fifteen years ago I "said" Mass facing a wall. Now I look into your eyes, over the Host. I used to give you "advice" (i.e., tell you what to do); now we have "counseling." Confessions were heard in a "box"; now, at least when it is pastorally necessary, it's done face-to-face. These are all healthy and positive developments. It's become much more personal, less "official" and abstract. But some of us older priests find it difficult to enter into the new role. We love you people, but it's going to be difficult to make the new ritual any different from what we've had. (And probably some of you will still want that zip-zip, over-and-out confession in the box.) Many of us are not yet emotionally ready to pray with you about your sinfulness, still less about ours. We have been raised in an atmosphere that placed great emphasis on the confessor as *judge*. True, the old books said the confessor was also to be a teacher and a doctor. But I'm afraid some of us priests "taught" rather formally and "doctored" quite impersonally.

But change we must. The ritual understandably directs the priest to "receive the penitent kindly." If the whole church is to be a sacrament of the love of Christ made visible, then priests, who are, in a sense, individual "sacraments" of the presence of Christ, will have to make confession a real sign of the personal, forgiving Christ. Give us time, and help us do it.

3. The need for prayer. The new ritual says: *"The priest and the penitent* are to prepare themselves for

8

the celebration of the sacrament *above all* by prayer." The priest should call upon the Holy Spirit for enlightenment and charity. The penitent should see his life in the light of the example and commandments of Christ and pray for the forgiveness of his sins.

It will make a tremendous difference if I (as priest or penitent) spend 10, 20, 30 minutes of simple, honest personal prayer before beginning the sacrament. Prayer in this case should not be an excessive concern only about what I am going to say or a time of hair-splitting worry or a fight with scrupulosity, but a realization of two things: God's love and my real sinfulness. I am a sinner, and I know I am a sinner. Otherwise I should be home polishing my homemade halo.

I am really guilty of at least a partial attitude of resistance to the friendship of God. I have hurt myself and others. *I cannot heal myself.*

But an infinitely tender God offers me his healing and mercy, renewal of my renewal and reconciliation, peace and strength.

I realize my dignity, I know my guilt. I believe in God's mercy, I accept my responsibility, I promise to let him repair and heal my life.

I see my life not as that of a highly ethical, natural man, doing what culture and society generally call for. My standard is Jesus. I am a "Christ-ist." There is only one standard whereby I am to judge my life — and that is Jesus' life and words.

If I am praying with the priest who will celebrate the sacrament with and for me, I realize that I am not an isolated individual. Even if the rest of the community is not present, I know that he is sent visibly by Christ and by the Body.

4. A need for wholeness, for seeing the complete picture. We have come out of what theologians call an "act-oriented" moral theology: that is, one that was more concerned with isolated external actions than interior intention and attitude. Theologians now are not denying that some "things" are seriously sinful; they are insisting that it is *whole persons* who sin, love, believe and betray.

What is even more important, they are insisting on what should be obvious: a person is one who thinks, understands and makes free choices. These free choices become an ongoing choice, as far as the direction of one's life is concerned. A girl marries a boy for life —because she loves him— *all the time.* A man becomes a doctor because he wants to be a doctor *all the time* — not totally committed to his calling one day, totally uninterested the next.

What has all this to do with the sacrament of reconciliation? The fact that just as sin is not an isolated action but a series of choices that have become an ongoing attitude, so also grace, love of God, penitence are ongoing. An act of contrition is not isolated from the rest of our life — we are presumably sorry in our whole person, in our whole life. Our sense of weakness, our trust in God's healing, our awareness of God's power is not the feeling of the moment but a feeling that is in our whole life.

So also, the particular celebration of the sacrament is not an isolated affair — it comes out of a spirit of penitence, trust and faith, *and it continues* after the celebration. Jesus does not "become present" only at Mass and during the celebration of penance. He is present *all the time* but becomes visibly present through the visible church's celebration of the sacraments. People in love, friends, husbands and wives love each other in their *whole* life. They must express this love visibly some of the time; they express it in intense personal ways only once in a while. But they love each other all the time.

So it is with God. He heals us all the time. He surrounds us with his forgiveness all the time. And our sorrow, faith, acceptance of healing are present all the time. It is, in a sense, a preparation for, or a continuation of, the high-point moment when the church "glows more brightly" for a moment in sacramental celebration.

We will be helped in our problems with confession (indeed, with our faith itself) if we can resist the temptation to isolate things, to separate our lives into disconnected acts that seem to have no bearing on each other. It is not realistic to split ourselves up into body, soul, mind, imagination, etc. We should not forget that, for good or ill, today is the fruit of all our yesterdays. No man is an island. And no part of our life should be considered an island.

The experience of community, leadership, prayer and wholeness. It is of the very nature of Christianity to strive to accept these gifts from God. Like everything else, this very process, too, is ongoing.

In this book we are attempting to analyze the fundamental ideas and attitudes which are presupposed for any meaningful celebration of the sacrament and without which any ritual, new or old, is useless.

OUTLINE OF RITUAL FOR ONE PENITENT

(See chapter VI for further treatment)

1. *The priest welcomes the penitent.*
2. *The penitent* (or priest and penitent both) *begins* with the **Sign of the Cross** and accompanying words.
3. *The priest encourages the penitent* to have trust in God. He has a choice of five texts (or his own words). The penitent answers **Amen.**
4. *The Word of God*, prominent in the new rite, is read (or said from memory) by the priest. Selections from the Bible stress the mercy of God and his call to conversion.
5. *The confession of sins.* If necessary, the priest is to help the penitent make a complete confession, give suitable counsel, encourage the penitent to true sorrow by recalling to his mind that the Christian is made new in the paschal mystery, dying and rising with Christ.
6. *The manifestation of contrition.* The priest asks the penitent to *express* his sorrow (already present before the sacrament). Thus the **Act of Contrition** is made a distinct part of the sacrament. It can be expressed in any way. The one suggested is like the traditional formula.
7. The *absolution* by the priest emphasizes the action of the Trinity. The penitent answers **Amen.**
8. *Proclaiming the praise of God.* Several alternatives are offered. This can be as short as one sentence, for instance, the words of Psalm 117: "Give thanks to the Lord for he is good," to which the penitent responds "**For his mercy endures forever.**"
9. Dismissal. The priest then "dismisses the reconciled penitent."

COMMUNAL CELEBRATION OF THE SACRAMENT

1. *The celebration begins with a song expressing trust in God's mercy.* The priest then *greets* the people. Examples given resemble those at the beginning of Mass.
2. The priest prays that the community may have the grace of genuine and fruitful penance. There is time for *silent prayer,* then a *prayer aloud by the priest.*
3. *The word of God is proclaimed.* There may be three readings, interspersed with silence, song or a responsorial psalm. If there is only one reading, it is taken from the Gospel. A homily follows.
4. *A time of silence for examination of conscience and a deepening of sorrow for sin.* The ritual notes that, according to the needs and capacities of the people present, the priest may use a litany-like prayer to aid in this examination. (E.g., "For our sins of pride, forgive us, Lord. For our neglect of prayer," etc.)
5. *The "rite of reconciliation" begins with a Confiteor-type act of contrition followed by a brief, litany-like series of prayers.* Several samples are given. The first set has to do with the attitude of the penitent, each verse answered by, "We beseech you, hear us."
6. *Those who wish now make their individual confession* to one of the priests assisting at the celebration and receive individual penance and absolution. The penitent responds with his personal "Amen."
7. *A "proclamation of praise of God's mercy" follows,* the whole assembly joining in a psalm, hymn or litany, for example, the Magnificat of Mary or a psalm expressing praise and thanksgiving (e.g., Ps. 135).
8. *The priest concludes with a prayer and dismisses the people* with a blessing.

Chapter II

The Heart of the Matter:
Reconciliation

"Go first and be reconciled to your brother."

I dreamt I found an ideal church. I felt completely at home. I had never been there before, but I was treated like a charter member. I did not speak to everyone that first night, but I had a feeling of being welcomed by everybody as if he or she alone had been appointed to do so.

Yet their kindness was not oppressive. I saw no crusading look in anyone's eye. I felt that if I had turned out to be Jack the Ripper or St. Francis of Assisi, their look would have been the same — a simplicity and openness to whatever might be my need or my gift, and a quiet willingness to wait until I was ready to reveal either. Their respect gave me a new feeling of value and — strangely — independence.

That's not the end of my dream, but let's come back to reality for a moment. The dream will ultimately show, I hope, the deepest meaning of the sacrament of reconciliation, confession. If it seems as if we are going from A to B by way of Z, there is some method in the madness.

Our problem, I think, is not "confession," but *church*. Only when we realize what it means to belong to the community of Christ will we see any reason for sacramental, visible healing and reconciliation.

Many people believe in God, and some people believe in sin. But too many people don't see that "church" has any real relationship to either. "Church" has come to mean organization more than community; a defensive (or offensive) army more than a Spirit-filled sacrament of healing and life; an idea rather than an experience; a set of laws rather than a way of life.

So also, confession may be either trivial or traumatic; an ordeal or a bothersome obligation; inexpensive psychiatry or ritual magic.

But hardly a "celebration."

There can be no meaningful and meant "celebration" of the "sacrament of reconciliation" unless *we*—not I—feel like celebrating. And if I feel like celebrating, there's only one way to do it — with others. There's something or someone we're *all* glad about.

Such a "celebrating community" is *church*. In the sacrament of reconciliation, we are celebrating the fact that there is Good News: the spirit of Christ is abroad on the earth and is destroying death and the devil, sin and slavery. He's doing it through the *visible* power and life of Jesus that rests in a community which is called church.

(Certainly, God can deal with individuals every-where on earth. A human father, with considerably more effort, could get food and clothing to his children scattered all over town. But it works better if they're all together in one home.)

But you can't just scoop 50 people off the street, push them into a building on Sunday morning and say "Celebrate!" If they were in no hurry to get home, they would gloriously and uproariously drink up your champagne in toasts to whomever and whatever. But if you didn't promise them free cham-pagne the following week, they wouldn't come back.

The question is not "Is it a sin to miss Mass?" but "Why should there be a group of celebrators? Why a group? What's to celebrate?"

And now that we've run into that dead end, let's go back to my dream. I confess I didn't tell every-thing. I implied that no one felt better than anyone else, just concerned for everyone else. But . . .

. . . There was someone else there named Jesus whom I didn't meet the first night because he was in the kitchen helping with the dishes when I came and later drove someone to the airport.

They said that to call him "Teacher" wasn't ex-actly right, since he was much more than that. "Director" or "Leader" didn't sound right either. He was just *there,* and they all recognized something in him that they had been looking for all their lives. He taught them things they already knew, and helped them do things they had always done. But when they listened and worked, they were walking in

17

a new world. Not a Disneyland or Oz, but the same old neighborhood with something new inside.

He was an unlikely leader, they said. He reported for a small newspaper, had no journalism degree. He had met some of them at the ball park, a few at the hospital, and one had written to complain about one of his by-lines.

When they met him, they said, they knew he was the most honest man in the world. They found themselves telling him about themselves, their kids, their work — then their anger, their sins and their despair. He didn't offer them very practical answers. He just listened so intently that they never stopped talking, and they didn't feel embarrassed at taking his time.

People started asking where they could come and talk to him, and that's how these meetings started. It was amazing how he could tell those simple stories that opened doors inside your heart and revealed the sunshine as it was on the first morning, and darkness as it is in hell.

I must say, though, you wouldn't win any prizes with the crowd that came. Mostly from the housing project, with some outpatients from Emerson — you know the kind of people who go *there* — and some members of a cycle gang called the Turks.

He just put his hands on people, and looked at them, and they were cured on the spot — an alcoholic, a little boy blind from birth, a pusher.

He told us about his Father. And when he said "my Father" you knew that he meant your Father too. The Good News was that the Father loved everybody on earth, not just the nice people. He wanted everybody to be with him. The world was not hopeless: the Father took care of sparrows and dandelions and he would take care of people too.

It was fascinating and a little scary — an ordinary man standing there and saying that if you believed in *him,* trusted yourself entirely to him, you would be right with the Father. You knew he was telling the truth; you felt it in your heart. When he looked into your eyes you felt power coming out — not threatening you, or overwhelming you, just available — to heal or destroy any rottenness in your heart or in the whole world.

One of the guys said, "You know, when I picked up that drunk on Second Street, I couldn't help feeling like he was the most important man in the world—it was like picking up, well, like picking *him* up—or any of us. Do you know what I mean?"

I knew what he meant, in my dream . . .

But coming back to reality again, it may be hard for us to realize that this is what *church* is all about. A group of people gathered around Jesus, possessed by him, yet perfectly free. Totally following him, yet each an individual doing his own work. Feeling like him when going to work or feeding a child, yet knowing that you're doing it to *him*. Respecting the individuality of each one, yet finding him in everyone.

The dream, I must admit, was an x-ray dream that showed only the goodness of the church. It was *real* church but not the whole picture.

My dream showed a *mature* church: but all of us are only on our way, *becoming mature*. Peaches and horses, azaleas and wine mature to a point where they are "finished." But human beings are always the pilgrims of eternity.

And we — or church — are not only maturing *towards* something, but are maturing *out of* something — childish selfishness, narrowness, spite, rebellion, laziness, vindictiveness. We seem to be clear ponds. But even clear ponds have slime on the bottom, and sometimes we're shocked when it gets stirred up and clouds the water.

And so we ourselves are not only church, we are enemies of the church, the community of brothers and sisters of Jesus. He came to bring us together, and we insist on rebuilding the tower of Babel and speaking as many selfish languages as there are people involved.

Confession, or the sacrament of reconciliation, is Jesus' visible way of healing the sinfulness that prevents the growth of the mature church. Sin tears away parts of his Body. In many "good" Catholics sin creates a listlessness or fever that makes them largely uninterested in the other members of the Body. We make a half-hearted effort to apologize to God directly — but we won't even shake hands with someone next to us at Mass. *That's* not religion. I go to God my way, you go your way.

And we keep building the tower of Babel even though it keeps falling down on us.

The church is always in need of healing, of coming together again, putting back the torn members of his Body, *reconciliation*. Before we can be the ideal church we must be the healed church, the reconciled table community — as individuals and as a group. "If you are offering your gift at the altar, and remember that your brother has something against you, go first and be reconciled to your brother and then come and offer your gift."

Certainly I must apologize to my Jewish brother, my atheist friend, before I can pray with Jesus. But even more urgently must I be reconciled as one who sat at the eucharistic table and then stole my *brother's* bread, or good name, or peace of mind. If any group in the world must be healed before it can operate, it is the church. The very meaning of church is "the assembly gathered into *one* by Christ." One in heart and intention, in giving and receiving. The prime prerequisite for church is to *become* church, i.e., to be continually reconciled to the unity Christ demands, to forgive and be forgiven. *"Then* come and offer your gift."

Our problem today seems to be that we feel little need of reconciliation because we have not deeply experienced community in the first place — the real church of the dream.

A real community wants nothing more than reconciliation of members who have hurt it or left it. And if it is a real community, I do not stay away in shame or fear if I am guilty. I am aware that, no matter what I did, I am only adding to the sorrow of the community by refusing to come back, to accept forgiveness and healing.

If it is a real community, it is the visible forgiving kindness of Christ. I can be absolutely certain that I will be received, welcomed, all things forgotten and forgiven. And I would know that *he,* in the person of the priest, is forgiving me through his community.

If the church is what it's supposed to be — the *visible* forgiving kindness of Christ — you would be absolutely certain that you would be received, welcomed, all things forgotten and forgiven, treated as if nothing had happened. And you would know that he is forgiving you through them.

This is the meaning of the sacrament. The whole church is by nature a sacrament of reconciliation. Jesus leaves a group of people who are his visible forgiveness. He forgives us through the ministry of reconciliation entrusted to that group. The priest we meet in the celebration of the sacrament is the representation of Christ, the Head of the Body.

Reconciliation, in God's plan — and therefore in reality — cannot be a private thing between God and me. He reconciles us to himself in his Son — and the visibility of his Son today is that community, that visible Body of his called church. He reconciles us to himself as individuals and as his Body. The community welcomes us "back" as a body, through the particular ministry of a priest. If the priest and I are alone, it is "officially" the whole church that is present.

Evidently, the meaning of reconciliation is most clear when the whole community comes together, each to be forgiven, each to forgive; to show each other, as individuals and as a body, the forgiving kindness of Christ; to feel his love coming — *as he intends it to come* — through other human beings; to be strengthened, given new hope and courage, by a meaningful and personal *sign-sacrament*.

The sacrament of reconciliation, in other words, will best be done if there is visible evidence of a greater sacrament, the living Body of Christ, the Second Sacrament, the church.

I can hear someone saying, "That's not the way it is in *my* church!"

May be. All the more reason why *I* need to be reconciled and reconciling, so that it is *our* church.

The Three Musketeers, once on the Index of Forbidden books, may be an unlikely source for Christian inspiration. But they had the right idea of community: "All for one and one for all."

Chapter III

Who Is the God We Reject?

We can know what sin is only if we know the goodness it spoils, and the good God who made that goodness. The less we know God, the less we know about sin.

If a baby girl is taken from her mother at birth and raised in isolation by stern male nurses, it will do little good to tell her that it's not "ladylike" or "motherly" to snarl and bite. If I don't know how Jesus loved, I can't keep the new commandment to love as he does.

It is remarkable how God sometimes gets left out of discussions on confession. We have a fine assortment of phrases that make forgiveness sound like something out of a vending machine. "Sins are forgiven by a perfect act of contrition" sounds like "Sodium and chloride make salt." "There's no obligation to go to confession if you don't have any mortal sin." "What should I say in confession?" "I really don't do anything wrong." Is God involved in any of these questions?

It's true that God is at the back of people's minds. But that seems to be the trouble: he's at the *back*. And sometimes that picture back there is pretty hazy, distorted, a really "false" god.

Does your God get angry? Is he "mad" at you sometimes? Do you feel that when you lose your job, or your baby dies, he's punishing you? Do you wonder if he "really" forgives you? Do you see him as a gruff octogenarian who has to be appeased and get his pound of flesh before he will take you off his black list? Do you have to persuade him by your prayers, supposing you can even get him to listen? Is he really so far away that you can't believe he's aware of you?

They could call Vatican III tomorrow and condemn every one of the above propositions.

Here's a list of possible "qualities" of God. On a sheet of paper, write down the numbers which indicate *your* idea of God.

1. Sympathetic	15. Enthusiastic
2. Remote	16. Old
3. Courteous	17. Forgiving
4. Stern	18. Official
5. Cheerful	19. Merciful
6. Busy	20. Emotionless
7. Hopeful	21. Kind
8. Impatient	22. Overwhelming
9. Tender	23. Loving
10. Happy	24. Demanding
11. Pitying	25. Concerned
12. Exasperated	26. Angry
13. Faithful	27. Compassionate
14. Punishing	28. Lenient

You probably realize by now that only the uneven numbers (except the 10th) represent the qualities of the real God; he simply cannot have the others.

All the qualities on this list are *human*. We will insist, in a moment, that half of them are in God, in the fullest possible way. He is tender, sympathetic, forgiving, etc. He is *not* ruthless, angry, etc.

But let's not make God into our own image, even if the image is a good one. God is not a "pal," to be treated like one of that old gang of mine. He must not be made into one of the more insipid "father" characters on TV — who will stand for anything from their kids, and stand for nothing themselves.

God is mystery. There is no image that will hold him, except Jesus, and Jesus is himself mystery, i.e., that which both reveals and hides. "He who sees me sees the Father," indeed; but not the Father as we will see him when the veil of faith is drawn away in eternity.

God is transcendent, the theologians tell us; that is, he cannot be captured in human language or thought. He is not just human goodness multiplied a billion times. He is *beyond, other, totally different, unique, unspeakable, incomprehensible.*

It was a wise law that forbade the Jews to make any graven images of God, because doing so might have led them to our serene and remote grand-fatherly figure who used to sit high atop the high altar. We all tend to make, not false gods, but our own image of the true God.

Yet, and this is but more of the mystery of God, this same absolutely *other* God is closer to us than

27

our own spirit. He is not "out there" even if he is beyond understanding. He is one in whom we live and move and have our being; he is closer to us — though distinct — than the air we breathe, the blood that flows in our veins, the deepest feelings of our hearts.

This mysterious God told Moses to take off his shoes before approaching the burning bush; he gave the commandments amid the awesome thunder and lightning on Mt. Sinai.

Yet this is the God who said, "Can a mother forget her infant, be without tenderness for the child of her womb? Even should she forget, I will never forget you" (Isaiah 49, 15).

Realizing then, that we cannot capture God in human terms, yet knowing that he has poured his whole being into a human heart — his and our own, we may profitably consider some of the "qualities" on the list above.

Punishment is self-inflicted. There is no one "in" hell who did not voluntarily and consciously choose hell, i.e., total and eternally frozen alienation from God. He doesn't "send" anyone to hell; they're already there. He does not take pleasure in the agony of people on the way to hell; from a cross he pleads to them to let him liberate them. Yet he will not take away the most precious gift he gives all men: freedom. He cannot *force* forgiveness and healing on free persons.

Punishment is self-inflicted. If a man drinks poison, he has a sick stomach, a terrible headache, or worse. The punishment is built into the sin. If you refuse to speak to someone, lie about him, write nasty notes to him, where does that cold, miserable feeling around your heart come from? Is someone else punishing you, or are you punishing yourself? When a man gradually stops loving his wife, and freezes in this selfishness, is his empty, meaningless life somebody else's fault?

God does not have to "send" punishment. If a stick could jump into the fire of its own choice, its blackened corpse would be its own punishment. If a glass could strike itself against the wall and be shattered, the penalty is contained in the act.

Punishment is built right into the sin itself. Punishment is the ruin of something beautiful and healthy that has been abused by human freedom. Hell is the attitude of self-destruction into which men gradually "set" like cement. [1]

There is indeed punishment, eternal hell and temporary purification. But punishment is built into our freely chosen sin.

It is not fair, then, to blame God for what our own sins have done. Jesus was once asked, after a tower fell and killed many people, whether those people were sinners. His answer was "Certainly not! But I tell you, you will all come to the same end unless you reform" (Lk. 13,5). The context of the

[1] In a much lesser way, "purgatory" is a state of being purified from the built-in punishment of reluctance, half-heartedness, the *momentum* of sin, all that *we* have accumulated by willing neglect over the years. God does not "burn" it out of us. He is not some sadist waiting until our pain reaches a certain degree of intensity before he "relents." Purgatory is the painful realization of how deep (though not fatal) our abuse of truth and love has been during life.

Gospel simply indicates that these people were not *more guilty* than others.

A false mentality has risen in many people. A baby dies, a husband gets cancer, there is a great financial loss. "I'm being punished for what I did when . . ." This is not fair to the God who loved the world so much that he gave his only Son. If we were to accept the logic of these people's feelings, we would have to say that, for a God who is all powerful, he's doing a poor job at taking revenge on his enemies. If he were really serious about being vindictive, he surely wouldn't do it so half-heartedly—a nice old woman here, a child there while thousands of crooks, hypocrites, adulterers, cheats, liars, thieves, tyrants have six-course dinners every night.

Well, what about the suffering of the innocent? We might as well admit it, the rational explanations of suffering do not help a mother whose child has just died. But let's try it anyway.

God does not give half-heartedly. He gives the best. So he gave us freedom, real freedom. Man can choose. He can choose life or death. He can choose to be enriched eternally by God, or he can decide to be his own god.

God wants to give the gift of freedom so strongly that he is willing to pay the price: the suffering that results from the abuse of freedom in both the sinner *and his victims*. God does not strike the sinner dead; instead, he comes himself to heal both the sinner and the innocent sufferers. The passion and death of Christ, ultimately, was the price God had to pay for giving freedom to man.

If a man takes a gun to kill another, God does not

stop the bullet. He himself comes — indeed has long since come — to bring the victim to himself. If the prodigal son wants his money to waste on debauchery, he gives him the money and then stands with open arms waiting to heal the misery the money will cause.

If God were to physically stop one bullet, he would logically have to stop all bullets. Ultimately he would have to stop all freedom.

But what of cancer, starvation, babies dying of malnutrition? Our explanation — and it is not overwhelming — is that evil in the world is the result of what man has done to the world. This baby in Bangladesh is not dying because his mother was sinful — but because the world is sinful. Our energy crisis and pollution crisis are examples — among many — of what man can do to the world, i.e., to the whole world, all people. Who is responsible for the sickness that comes from polluted atmosphere? Who is responsible for the fact that a father kills his child in a Calcutta slum?

These are rational explanations. They are true, and some of them are forceful. But they will do little for the mother holding a dead baby in her arms, or the man whose wife is dying of cancer.

The only practical "answer" is Jesus. He is God's response to all the evil and suffering in the world: *he comes to plunge himself into our suffering* and thus to heal it. God so loved the world that he gave everything he possessed to save it without destroying man's freedom to love.

We must never think of God "over there" send-

31

ing us crosses and almost daring us to get up the steep hill carrying them to him. That *is* blasphemy. God is on *our side* of suffering, giving us courage to maintain hope and love and faith in him.

Is God Angry?

It is true that the Bible speaks of the wrath of God. Jesus said that our Father will treat us as we have treated others in not forgiving. As with descriptions of God as punishing, we must take these expressions as *human* ways of talking about the absolute holiness of God. He is simply *good*. He cannot be "lenient" in the sense of caring nothing about the sickness of soul or body that infects his children. God can no more tolerate sin that "dry" can at the same time be "wet," or "plus" can be simultaneously "minus," or heat tolerate cold. In human life, we can "mix" these things. Mix ice cream and hot coffee and you get a tepid mess. But there is no "mixing" in God. He is absolutely pure. He *must* want to cure the sickness, heal the fever, recreate the dead, free the imprisoned heart. He simply cannot deny his own nature and say that evil is not evil. He loves the sinner as only God can love — with the undying love that will not tolerate harm to his beloved.

God cannot be angry because anger implies a lack of control. We are angry when our will is thwarted, or some evil is sticking in us that defies our power. But there is no evil that has power over God. His infinite might destroyed evil, sin and death by submitting to it on a cross. The world, good and bad, is in his hand.

Remote?

God is indeed an "awe-ful" God — but this transcendence does not carry him a million miles away. "My ways are not your ways," indeed; but God lives within "our ways." He is majestic, but not like the distant Rockies, inaccessible and frozen.

God cannot be remote in the sense of being aloof, haughty, uncaring, "official." The paradox of God is that he is infinite and yet deals with the here-and-now — actual people, real situations — with infinite tenderness and care. We cannot imagine this, since our experience deals with things that have limits and quantity. For us, the bigger things get, the more limited the personal aspect: General Motors doesn't weep for anybody, and ITT hasn't the least tug of a heartstring about the fact that Jimmy Jackson flunked algebra.

God is, in fact, the only one who *can't* be remote, since his loving and sustaining care holds everything in being, even the speckles on a trout.

Our scientifically brainwashed minds see God as winding up the watch of the world and letting it run. Not true. He does let the nature of *things* take its course — gravity, atomic energy, light, etc. But the nature of persons is that they be like God — *free, loving, aware, concerned, healing.* If the tree would fall into nothingness without God to sustain it, how much more would our fragile intelligence and freedom. Spirit cannot store up food, like a plant. It needs to be held in existence most delicately at every moment, like a baby receiving a transfusion. And this is God's constant personal providential love!

Man's abuse of freedom is part of the risk God took, not something happening beyond his control. Evil has been radically defeated in the death and resurrection of Christ. It lives on, like the "green" leaves of a fallen tree, with a power that is only apparent. God's "anger" and revenge was to destroy evil by letting it "destroy" him on the cross and waste all its energy in so doing. He absorbed it into himself and rid the world of it.

But Isn't God Terribly Busy?

Remember the whimsical TV program that showed God's switchboard lighted up with thousands of contradictory requests — for rain and dry weather, one for Farmer Brown and the other for the Kiwanis picnic; victory for both Notre Dame and Southern Methodist; first place for all nine ladies in the pie-baking contest. With a whole world to run, how can God have time for me — or, happy thought, even to notice my sins?

One answer is to look at what we very limited creatures are able to manage in this matter of "busyness." Look around you. Do you see people with hundreds of friendships, each one never far from the edges of their consciousness? If a limited human being can never really be too "busy" for anyone, what of the infinite God who is subject to no problems of time, space, energy, knowledge or love?

God doesn't just hold millions of people in *mere* existence — as if they were so many plants in a vast garden. God maintains an individual relationship with each person. There is no one else in the world

34

like you. God surrounds you — the unique you —
with his love. He knows you *as you,* and simply offers
himself, according to your changing needs, as friend.
He is not even, as the song says, "just a prayer *away.*"
He's never away.

Overwhelming?

Doesn't God, after all, come on so strong that we
really have no choice? Isn't it all arranged? Aren't
we all programmed?

This may be the greatest mystery of all: God
makes us free and leaves us as free as he can. "As he
can" is not a restriction. It simply means that God
must do everything he can to *persuade* us to choose
happiness, health, love, fulfillment. He doesn't leave
us to blind choice. But he leaves enough wrappings
on his gifts that we do have to trust; he leaves room
for us to grow — by everyday choices — whose long-
range results are not evident at the moment.

Love is free. If it were an uncontrollable attraction, it would be merely physical or chemical. Love
is proven to be love when there is another attraction
which can be declined only at a price. Freedom
works toward unseen goals, and love is a decision
made both in darkness and in light. God wants no
ventriloquist-dummy children. Like a good parent,
he wants his children; but, unlike human parents,
there must be something more: his children must
want *him.* He has given us more than enough reason
to trust him; but trust him we must. He leaves us in
enough darkness that his gift of faith can make us
real persons.

35

What About an Emotionless God?

All right. If God isn't angry, or stern, or punitive, must we not also say that he is without all the "good" feelings too?

The catechism said God is unchangeable. The very nature of emotion is that it comes and goes; it is "high" and "low." Is it reasonable to think of God as a passionate lover, a zealous worker, a courageous martyr, an artist carried away by his song? Isn't that the very nature of emotion: it "carries us away"? But God must always be in control, cool, careful and restrained.

What does God have to control? The danger of loving too much? What must he be careful of? Making a mistake, getting hurt, taking the wrong turn, being fooled?

God is infinite goodness who has absolute power to do what love calls him to do. And what he does he does in compliance with his own first commandment—with his *whole* heart.

In us, of course, emotion is partly physical. It is quantitative. Not so in God. Joy, love, satisfaction, delight, sympathy are all in God in a way that does not depend on outward circumstances. These are names for his infinite breathing forth and receiving back — himself, in the love of the Trinity.

We need not worry about God's not being emotional. Whatever danger our feelings run, he is in no danger. Our worry should be that we do not make God emotional enough. Remember: "When Israel was a child I loved him . . . . It was I who taught him to walk . . . . I fostered them like one who raises an infant to his cheeks; yet, though I stooped to feed my child, they did not know that I was their healer" (Hosea 11, 1-4).

All the good that emotion does in our lives — the tremendous voltage of loving and striving, the unending forgiveness, the incredible patience, is supremely and infinitely present in God.

Can God be Compassionate?

If his loving support maintains our every muscle and heartbeat, every thought and judgment, every emotion and passion, he must be aware of every feeling we have. Being God, how can he not suffer with us?

Some will immediately object that God cannot suffer. True, God cannot be limited, and suffering is limiting. It means being constrained, prevented, hemmed in by a power bigger than ourselves. In that sense God cannot be as sad as we are, as angry as we are, because the essence of these feelings is a certain helplessness.

But insofar as compassion means loving someone so much that his suffering becomes our suffering, God's love is in us.

We must preserve the absolute freedom of God. He did not have to make the human race. But once he decided to make children, it would seem very probable that he would have to go all the way for them and *become limited. That is exactly what he did in Jesus.*

37

Forgiving, Merciful, Lenient

The Bible is the story of God's attempt to forgive his people, heal them, change them into healthy, loving, happy children. Forgiveness does not mean that God gets "mad," then decides not to take revenge after all, then says, "I'll love you, even if you're not worth it."

Forgiveness means that *we* change, not God. We need the sign of God's forgiveness, and we need to give a sign to others that we are sorry, and they need to do the same. But the sign of confession is not a sign that God has come around to deciding to give us pardon. God's forgiveness is his constant reaching out to us to enfold us again to himself, like the father of the Prodigal Son.

The word "mercy" originates in two Latin words, "miser" and "cor" — "miserable" and "heart." I am heartsick over someone's misery, injury, pain. I am com-passionate, I suffer with them.

Again we must say that God does not suffer in the sense of being deprived of something he cannot get, or being thwarted by a superior power. In that sense he is not affected as we are. But the heart of compassion, mercy, and forgiveness is the overflowing desire to heal, to sympathize, to create and recreate goodness, health, happiness. God is sym-pathetic, and com-passionate.

God easily forgives. He does not demand his pound of flesh. He is more willing to forgive than we are to be forgiven. But he cannot be indifferent to truth and justice, right and faithfulness. As we have said, he can no more tolerate sin than dry can tolerate wet, or plus tolerate minus. He is love, pure and simple, and there can be no approval of anything but truth.

In forgiving, God does not say, "It really isn't important that you sinned, hurt yourself and others, damaged your person with malice." Rather he says, "I want to heal the damage you have done to yourself. It is sickness, death. It is actual, real tragic. I cannot tolerate injury to any of my children."

This is the God we offend by our sinfulness. If we know him, we know what sin is. If we choose to make him an unreasonable, uninterested, distant God, we are in the atmosphere where sin festers.

It reminds one of the old saying, "Nothing succeeds like success." The more I open myself to experiencing this mysterious loving God, the more I will experience the shame, stupidity, insolence, thanklessness of sin. The more I close myself off to facing this ever-present friend, the more I am able to rationalize my sin. "The fool said in his heart, 'There is no God.' "

Jesus, the Sacrament of God

Once there was a man who said, "Philip, he who sees me sees the Father." If God wanted to communicate with us, he had to speak our language. *Because* God wanted to communicate his healing life to us, he entered into our actual human condition of misery. "He emptied himself, and took the form of a slave, being born in the likeness of men . . . he humbled himself, obediently accepting even death — death on a cross!" (Phil. 2,7-8)

Jesus is the living sign (i.e., sacrament) of the living, loving, healing God. He is the "first" Sacrament.

We have tried to see that our human feelings are somehow transcendently in God. They are actually present in God-made-man, Jesus. The tremendous fact about Jesus is that when we hear his words, have him touch us, sit and eat with him, we are hearing and feeling and touching God — our Brother God, who shows us the One Father God and his Spirit of love.

When he spoke to the paralytic, "Your sins are forgiven"; when he told the adulteress to go home in peace; when he embraced Simon after the resurrection — he was being the *visible sacrament of reconciliation*. No other sign or sacrament was needed. They were in contact with the sacrament of God, Jesus.

Jesus Today

Today, Jesus is perfectly human, and perfectly freed from the limitations he was willing to suffer on earth to share our lot. The Risen Jesus no longer has a need to be angry as he had to be on earth; he cannot be sad, because as man he sees the eternal victory, the perfect healing of all who are willing to receive it—the millions of the past, the millions yet unborn. He will never have to lay down his life again, or pass through the darkness of death. He has taken all our human ills and destroyed them by letting them destroy him.

He is the God who deals with us in the same way

40

that he dealt with us in his own mortal life — by words and actions, by visible appearance, by love that we can feel and hear and taste, by forgiveness that is as palpable as that given to the adulterous woman.

How?

Let's go back to the ideal community we thought about in the second chapter. The church is all we can see of Christ today. And what we must see in the church is the forgiveness of Christ. The business of the church — all of us — is to say to each other and to the world: "If you wish to know how Christ loved and healed, we will show you. Even if you don't wish to know him, we must show his love and forgiveness."

There is no use insisting that people need signs or sacraments when they insist that they don't. If someone finds confession a bore or an ordeal or a meaningless ritual, it is obviously not a sacrament in the sense of a living meaningful sign of the forgiving God and the loving Jesus. (Whose fault this is, if anybody's, is another question.)

So the church — all of us — has the vocation of being the sacrament of Christ's visible healing. We, the church, ought to be such a loving community that those who alienate themselves from God by sin will be attracted to the forgiveness and healing that is obviously available in such a Christlike group.

This is the problem and the potential of the sacrament of reconciliation. Reconciliation cannot be forced on people, it must be irresistibly offered. Sacraments cannot be said to mean something to people when they do not, in fact, mean much at all to them. They must be convincing and attractive signs of the loving Father, the ever-present Christ, given by the only thing that is visible of Christ today — his Body, the loving church.

The new ritual will be a vehicle of divine compassion if there is real church — a community of loving Christians and priests who appreciate their own special sacramentality, that of being the visible sign of Jesus himself.

It is easy to say, "Well, our parish is not that way, so the ritual will be just some more rigamarole there." It is still worse to say, "I will withdraw into an elite group where the real Church lives."

We are the problem and we are the answer. The church is the ideal sign of the forgiving Christ — and it is his suffering Body, constantly fighting off the strangling tentacles of sin. Every day the church has to start over — fighting the perverted impulse to withdraw, to be a stranger. Every day you and I (the church) have to open ourselves to reconciliation— within our own mixed-up selves, with all our brothers and sisters and *their* mixed-up selves, and with the ever-waiting, loving Father.

Only Jesus, God and man, can "put it together." He is the sign of the union of God and man. He is reconciliation.

We are the problem and the answer. We are all a caravan following Christ. We detour, we turn back, we fall by the wayside. We take turns being self-defeating. Yet there is always the Body, waiting to welcome us back. And we are part of the welcoming committee.

"I was a stranger — lost with the losers, the alie-

nated, the self-punishers — and you took me in."
"And I was the one who took *you* in."

Chapter IV

Fatal and
Not-Yet-Fatal Sinfulness

A world-renowned psychiatrist, Karl Menninger, has written a book entitled *Whatever Became of Sin?* He is echoing thousands of parents who wonder whether their children have any consciences. The church itself is accused of contributing to the general permissiveness of today's society.

Mother's say to teachers, "Make the children learn their prayers; tell them what is wrong and what is right." Fathers probably say, "Teach the kid not to steal butter in the supermarket and leave the love stuff till later."

But teachers — and the theologians they read — insist: "Sin is not a single theft here or an isolated adultery there. Love is not just a half hour on Sunday or the morning offering before the bathroom mirror. By its very nature, sin (as well as love) is an attitude, an ongoing attitude, a spirit that tends to pervade one's whole life. In the case of sin, it's like an infection that fills the blood stream, even though its results are seen in only one boil. In the case of love, it's an energy in the heart all the time, popping to the surface in different, *but not isolated,* ways."

So what?

So it is important that the boy (and his father) not steal butter in the supermarket. But it is more important that they have a strong positive reason *all the time* for not stealing anything from anybody; a reason that drives them to be concerned about justice for all.

One life isn't important, some say. What's the harm of stealing a towel or two? No one is really hurt, and I'm not going to do anything *big*. But if I am really willing to steal or lie, I am already comfortable with untruth, injustice, sin. I am allowing an infection to enter my overall (supposedly upright) attitude. At the very least, I am not taking God with total seriousness: I am entering upon a "what's the least I have to do?" attitude which hardly fulfills the commandment about loving God with our whole heart.

"It's the spirit that counts" is as true of sin as it is of making birthday gifts for mother or fighting for a hopeless cause. Too long we have taken refuge in a *list* of sins, even in the Ten Commandments taken as a minimum set of things I can teach a child and thus fulfill my obligation to "make" him into a Christian. There are thousands of people who can recite the Ten Commandments backward and forward, but who (for reasons they justify) see nothing wrong with being prejudiced against blacks, or whites, charging whatever the market will bear, doing seven hours work in eight, or hating relatives for life over a disputed inheritance. The 10 sentences of the Ten Commandments aren't all there is to morality: Jesus said it involves loving others as he did — and there's no end to that.

Theologians [1] today speak of the "fundamental option" whereby we *gradually* come to terms with God's call to live the life of Jesus. There are only two choices. Either we gradually open ourselves and grow to a *way of life* that accepts Jesus as the Alpha and the Omega of our life, the basis of all decisions, the goal of all love, the power that motivates all actions; or we gradually close ourselves to any basic relationship with God; we gradually set, like cement, in a selfish attitude; we do not accept the fact that Jesus is the only source of salvation, still less make it a matter of faith and love; we slowly succumb, knowingly and willingly, to spiritual death.

The Ten Commandments are indeed important, in fact essential. But Jesus calls for a spirit that covers our whole life and imitates his love in all situations, not just the obvious ones indicated by the Ten Commandments. The Sixth Commandment, for instance, tells a man what he may *not* do; it does not specify how he is to love his wife: whether today, for instance, he should bring up a matter that is irritating him, or postpone talking about it until a more favorable time, or just forget it all together and take her out to dinner. No list of rules, no matter how long, can tell him precisely what he should do in this situation. He must decide, must make his decision

[1]Cf. Bernard Haering, *Sin in the Secular Age,* for much of the material of this chapter.

out of a careful look at the circumstances of the moment, motivated by a spirit of love that is always present and always growing, basically the same and yet open to new depths.

"Thou shalt not kill"? Only with a spirit centered on and nourished by Jesus can I realize that I must not only refrain from killing, but that I must promote and protect life all the time, in a thousand ways. The circumstances will be constantly changing—but the attitude, the spirit with which I foster life will be constant.

It is my *spirit* that can be good or evil, and the deep root of all love or sin. The opposite of being open to the Spirit of Jesus all the time is a gradual hardening into a frame of mind, attitude, which becomes a *way of life*, an attitude, for instance, that will get every possible pleasure out of life without thinking of others, and being restrained only by the pressure of others' opinion or a respectability needed to maintain my position in society.

As theologians recently have emphasized, nobody coldbloodedly goes into mortal sin with "full knowledge and full consent." To be a sinner is to be a coward besides. Nobody ever admitted he was "turning away from God." We back into sin, disguise our intentions, lie to ourselves, rationalize. "This time doesn't count. I've had such a hard day, or life. Others don't understand. I really haven't the will power. God surely wouldn't forbid . . . ."

The fatal attitude that grows in the dark, the gradual hardening of a person into a law unto himself, is called mortal, *or fatal,* sin. It's all there, on the inside, like a cancer that has been growing for months before the first pain is felt. It can be expressed externally in one way or another — murder, adultery, stealing, slander — and each of these is terribly wrong. But to the overall inner attitude, there is little moral difference between them. The Ten Commandments indicate the *obvious* evil ways in which the inner attitude of sinful independence is expressed. There are countless other ways: making life miserable for others precisely by *not doing* anything, and then using that as an excuse: *"I* didn't do anything!" Or, maintaining an external image as the observer of all laws — yet doing all the right things for the wrong reasons.

Ultimately, because of the overall influence of this attitude, our life is either-or: either one of faith and love, a way of life given over to God *all the time*—as a lover is given over to the beloved all the time, even when he is busy mowing the lawn or finessing his opponent's king; *or* is one of total (though well-disguised) selfishness, a way of life given over to self *all the time,* God being really but obliquely ignored, as a thief is on the lookout for opportunity all the time, whether he is walking in to church or wandering through a store.

It is possible to overdo anything, of course, and we may be in danger of going to the opposite extreme from an act-centered morality, i.e., one that concerned itself only with isolated sinful acts, not the deep spirit beneath them. But a doctor does not merely treat symptoms (the acts): red face, headache, shortness of breath, high blood pressure. He goes deeper, and finds the one inner cause of all these disorders.

Sins or Sins?

Those who want something definite will be happy to know that the new ritual has an appendix with suggestions for an examination of conscience. There are one or two hundred *ways* to sin — *acts* — listed.

But they are all listed under three fundamental questions about attitude, spirit, way of life: 1. "The Lord said, 'Love the Lord your God with your whole heart.'" 2. The Lord says, 'Love one another as I have loved you.'" 3. Christ the Lord says: 'Be perfect as the Father is perfect.'"

The first question under the latter heading is: *"What is the fundamental direction of my life?"*

It is this deep, ongoing attitude — good or bad — that we should see as our greatest concern. This may be expressed in a single action. The sins listed under the Ten Commandments ordinarily cause such damage to the community that no one who is adult and morally developed can ignore the fact that he is willfully separating himself from God.

Yet, as a great modern theologian says, not every act of man expresses the total person. Mortal sin, as fundamental option, happens only when the act rises from the depths of conscience, and reveals man's fully accountable abuse of liberty — a choice that truly expresses his whole existence. Most of the relatively free acts of man do not express his whole self, but they do contribute in one direction or another to a person's total self-determination (Cf. B. Haering, *Sin in the Secular Age,* p. 184).

It is the direction or drift of our lives that counts. For sooner or later this direction becomes a way of life — faith or mortal sinfulness.

Some will object that, while sin is indeed gradual, faith seems to come with a "peak experience" of Jesus, *after which* growth is gradual. They point to the many Catholics (rash judgment?) who don't seem to be going *any place,* in virtue or sin, but who suddenly "meet Jesus."

It does seem possible for people to remain in an almost childish condition, morally speaking, for a long time, leading non-moral lives. They may awaken to the need to decide only late in life.

But from then on, the growth is still gradual. It is not once-and-for-all, as Jesus pointed out in the parable about the seed that fell on shallow soil; and, on the other side of the ledger, in the parable about the son who first said No to his father but ultimately said Yes for good (Mt. 21, 28-32).

Fatal sin, then, no matter when it starts, is the result of a gradual process, whereby a person becomes his own measure of morality.

Mortal sin is, no matter how indirectly, and cowardly, a refusal of God's friendship. Deliberately not to accept God's gift is to refuse it. It may take many years for the refusal to become final, but it is still refusal.

Fatal sin is a fundamental option against God, no matter how horrendous that phrase sounds, and how unthinkable for any reasonable person. But to seek other good things at the expense of God's good things, and to make this a way of life, is a life option, a fundamental one. The things chosen are good—pleasure, power, prestige, comfort, success—but they are chosen with an eye closed to the use of them for the honor of God.

Mortal sin means total alienation from God, from the community, and from self. I have many friends — as long as I can do it "my way," as long as friendship does not cost me anything I really value. I am really a stranger in a phony paradise. I know I am a stranger to God, because I haven't taken the time to know him. And sooner or later my psychiatrist will tell me that I am alienated from myself.

The words of Francis Thompson, in *The Hound of Heaven,* come to mind:

> I fled him, down the nights and down the days;
> I fled him, down the arches of the years;
> I fled him, down the labyrinthine ways
> Of my own mind, and in the mist of tears
> I hid from Him, and under running laughter.

Mortal sin is ultimately idolatry, that funny sin that nobody commits any more. My god is my own egotism. I come first, and I have convinced myself that this is the only way to go, and it's reasonable to my carefully conditioned mind.

The conclusion is not that we have nothing to worry about, since nobody in his right mind could be so blind to his faults — but that we should worry more about the drift of our lives in *not-yet-fatally-sinful attitudes* — all that has trivialized as "only venial sin."

Again Father Haering: Real sins of weakness are one thing: a minor detour, a slip by people who are sincerely on the road to conversion, who are guilty only of a slight unwarranted hesitation as they travel the right path.

Sinfulness of this kind does not (at least not yet) represent an attitude that has settled in. It is a momentary lapse into a former habit — sarcasm, exaggeration, mistrust, a domineering spirit. It is regretted as soon as it is done.

But not-yet-fatal sinfulness (venial) can be quite another thing. It is progressive deterioration — the only way anyone ever went to the total attitude of mortal sin. It is, for all practical purposes, the absence of any real intention to return to previous fervor. It is the rather conscious ignoring of the need to pray, to make peace, to admit wrong, to cooperate. At the same time there is a naive justification of the fact that one is not guilty of mortal sin because those three famous conditions have not been met.

No need to exaggerate. It is possible for such a person not to go all the way to mortal sin — possibly out of fear, possibly because of the fact that there is a basic love of God. But such a life will still be stunted, incomplete like that of a man who is always in poor health. It hardly corresponds with the picture of Christian living found in the Gospels.

It is worth worrying about.

What Do We Mean When We Sin?

Real sinfulness is an approach to total self-centeredness — or the arrival at that depth of human misery. Sin says — never directly, of course — that I am the center of the world: everyone and everything else, insofar as I can manage, must defer to my wishes. Yet my wishes are never satisfied, and I sink deeper into anger at myself and others, loss of hope, rationalization, frantic attempts to prove that I really am happy.

I am incensed at the arrogance of others, but I am capable of the supreme arrogance of all: denying God the right to be adored and loved with my *whole* being. I don't really deny that God deserves worship. Of course he does. But of a certain kind. I put in my appearance at church quite regularly, and everybody knows I am not like the rest of men — murderers, adulterers, gangsters and drug-pushers. I merely seek a good life for myself.

Sin is ultimately refusal of friendship with God. God becomes irrelevant. He is not important, because I am so important. I can't have two masters, and it's my choice to be absorbed in the hard work of having my own good time.

What I am really doing in my sinful attitude is rejecting responsibility. It's too much, it's not my fault, other people are worse than I am, surely God doesn't expect all this. Am I my brother's keeper?

All without doing anything. Most sinfulness is omission. I choose not to see any reason for *growing* ("I learned my religion in grade school") to greater awareness of who God is, of what other people need and suffer, of what I am capable. It is the omission of thankfulness. Why all the to-do about thanking God. He really owes us all we need, doesn't he?

Sin is not being there to do the good that is obviously called for — encouragement and patience with children; willingness to communicate with husband or wife; listening to the frightened adolescent or the pompous neighbor. "I was hungry, and you did not give me to eat."

Sin is failing to follow one's best (but fading) convictions. "I'll get around to it some time." Sin is gradually being locked into one's own egotism, freezing into distortion the image of a free and intelligent God he put within us.

Sin is hiding our talent in the ground instead of letting others have the benefit of it, avoiding the pain of possible failure, misunderstanding or rejection. It means a very calculating effort *not* to carry a cross every day.

Finally, worst of all, sin contains its own punishment within itself. Hell is people who have frozen into selfishness. The man who does not forgive gradually corrodes his own ability to forgive. The woman who lets the acid of envy or resentment drip on her heart ends up by having no heart of her own. The person who runs riot in the name of freedom becomes the slave of his own passion. If he cannot rejoice in the good of others, he soon finds no good to rejoice about in himself. If he is not interested in truth and beauty, he becomes less than human, that is, he gradually loses the most human of qualities, the innate desire to know truth and embrace goodness.

Sin is allowing — again, usually omission — a jungle of slavery and alienation, darkness and decay grow over what might have been a city set on a hill.

Sin Is Social

"I'm not hurting anyone else," says the man who gets drunk, the girl who takes drugs, the woman who doesn't pray, or the couple who decide to live together before marriage.

As in the argument about which came first, the chicken or the egg, it is difficult to know whether sin begins with hurting my neighbor or hurting myself. If I am willing to damage myself and let friendship with God cool, I will scarcely be concerned about anyone else. On the other hand, I am sinful precisely to the degree that I refuse to accept my neighbor, for if I do not love the brother I can see, St. John says, I certainly do not love the God I cannot see.

In any case, sin is social. At the very least, my sinful attitude, because it damages *me,* makes me less able to give you the love to which you have a right. For God sent me to be concerned about your needs and your pain. He is hungry and homeless in you, in prison, a stranger. I am sent to give you the food of acceptance and support, forgiveness and healing. I am sent to do what I can to release you from whatever prison of sin or neurosis, poverty or injustice, you are in. I am sent to make this world a home for you. I *am* your keeper, my brother, my sister.

But if I let this gray sickness blight my spirit, I cannot do for you the good of which I *would* have been capable. I am like the basketball player who has let himself get out of condition. He is playing the game, he is not making any obvious errors — but he is not the player he could be — and he is doing an injustice to his teammates.

You may not even know what you are missing. You take the miserable gift I give you, grateful for scraps, thanking me for my generosity, never suspecting my potential.

Sin, therefore, diminishes my ability to pull my weight in the community. "He's doing the best he can," the kind people say, but I know that I am not. I am gradually breaking away from the solidarity that should characterize the Christian community, the family. It's not that I refuse to speak to you — I cross the street a block away. It isn't that I want to hurt you, it's just that I never arrive with the medicine.

Sinfulness blunts my concern for the community of Christ, waters down any feeling I might have had about the need, in St. Paul's words, to "build up the Body of Christ in love."

(To repeat: When and if and because the church is a forgiving church-community, I will be drawn and attracted, not shamed, into accepting the healing of all this distortion, and I will again take my responsible place in the community circle.)

Sin has not only to do with the church, but with the world. Sin also means that I care little for the world. What has been called the "sin of the world" is the vast network of evil — like an enveloping mass of polluted air, that encompasses mankind. Where did it come from? Physical pollution comes from a million exhaust pipes and factory smokestacks. Moral pollution comes not only from Adam but "inasmuch as we have all sinned." It grows from the accumulated selfishness of mankind — yours, mine. Every mean word, every theft of another's peace, every selfish abuse of another's body or spirit, leaves a trace of poison in the moral atmosphere. Every time I destroy something in me by sin, I subtract from the world's supply of healing and hope. As I freeze up in isolation, the world is poorer for the lack of what I might have given. As my mind darkens, someone else does not see the light they would have seen in me. [2]

Can We Use that List of Sins in the New Ritual?

So much for the inner meaning of sin. Before we try to summarize what God wants to do in us to heal our sinfulness, we should note a danger in the "attitude" approach.

If, on the one hand, we can become too act-oriented, too concerned with isolated external actions without seeing the inner spirit that joined them, it is also possible to go too far in the opposite direction and become too attitude-oriented. We may be in danger of loving all men in general and not loving anyone in particular; of hating all sinfulness without hating this and that particular sin; trying to heal the whole spirit without putting medicine on any part of it.

Some will object to the inclusion of a long "ex-

[2]Father Haering lists the following particular forms of social sin: the refusal to join all men of good will who want to work for a better world; individualism blinding man to his social responsibilities; not working for reconciliation and peace at all levels; an unjust and merciless attitude toward one's neighbor, especially the poor; letting economics determine the social structure of all life; the refusal to cooperate in the better distribution of earthly goods; a totally profit-oriented economy; consumerism creating artificial needs and wants; the hypocrisy and lying of the overprivileged and powerful; keeping social structures which continue injustice; manipulation of public opinion; one culture imposing itself on another; racism.

58

amination of conscience" in the new ritual, fearing it will only confirm people in an act-oriented extrinsic morality.

Yet the list can be used with profit — and the ritual does merely "propose" it, presuming "completion and adaption" according to local custom and the variety of persons who may use it.

It should be noted that the list emphasizes three great areas, corresponding to the commandment that comes before all others: "Love the Lord with your whole heart, and your neighbor as yourself."

All sinfulness springs from our neglect in these three areas, and our guilt can be healthily unmasked by concentrating on them:

1) *Love of God:* This section begins with the question of fundamental option: "Is my heart directed to God so that I truly love him above all things in the faithful observance of his commandments, as a son loves his father? Or am I more concerned about temporal things? Do I have a right intention in my actions?"

2) *Love of neighbor:* Again the emphasis is on the general attitude. "Do I have true love of my neighbor, or do I abuse my brothers for my own ends, or treat them in a way I would not like to be treated?"

This section also speaks of sharing my goods with those who are poorer than I, defending the oppressed, helping those in need — the poor, the weak, the old, strangers, people of different races. It recalls the mission received in confirmation, and the needs of church and world, to be worked and prayed for, e.g., unity of the church, evangelization, serving justice and peace.

We are reminded to be concerned about the welfare of the human community in which we live, of serving society with love.

3) *Loving ourselves:* This section begins with a question about the "fundamental direction of my life"; in other words, the attitude, spirit, fundamental option, drift of my whole life, for it is here that sin or faithful love is found. Am I trying to be a free son or daughter of God; free, that is, *from* enslavement to my own selfishness; free *for* opening myself to God?

Chapter V

Putting It All Together

The great danger in ritual is *ritualism,* excessive concern for externals. The pitfalls of *enthusiasm,* on the other hand, are a certain *anti-sacramentalism* and self-guidance by "inner light." Rugged religious *individualism* sees no need for church, community, priests and "rigamarole." At the other extreme, "community spirit" can be used to bludgeon the members into a conformity they do not feel. Hell-and-damnation preaching can (or could) produce scrupulosity. Theological explanations of fundamental option may produce a certain laxity about the actual details of living the Christian life.

It should be no surprise that the sacrament of penance is one of the most vulnerable of Catholic practices, because so many crucial elements of Christian life converge on it.

Having considered some of the major presuppositions of an authentic celebration of the sacrament — community, God, sin — what can we do, practically, to use the new ritual in a healthy, helpful way?

A Loving God Is Our Only Hope

If there is one sentence that sums up the Bible, it is: "God is love, and he who abides in love abides in God, and God in him" (I John 4, 16). Life is a hell without the conviction that there is a loving God at the heart of all things. Hell is rejecting that conviction while being perfectly aware that it is true.

The church, the sacraments, indeed all life is meaningless unless we have a fundamental and operating consciousness that God is love, unchanging love, and that his love is for me as well as all other men and women. All signs — street signs, hand shakes, letters, sacraments, Jesus — must be signs that say, "There is good news. You have a Father that gives you all he has. There is a Spirit of love all about you — within you, if you open yourself. There is healing in a human brother-God, Jesus. There is reason to trust, to believe, to hope. Listen."

If we do not start with this, we do not start. The gift to do so is available to us. The depth of our sacramental celebrations — Mass and confession — will depend on how seriously we choose to begin.

I Am Guilty of Sin

Only in the face of this loving God, am I able to admit my real guilt. All the rationalizations and self-pity, the excuses and the deliberate blindness, fall away in the presence of the humble love of God in Jesus. I admit that I need healing. I may be considered a moral leper or a pillar of the church, but I am a sinner. I don't know about others. I know that I am still partially or largely selfish, proud, weak, self-centered, self-indulgent, uncooperative, untrue, unloving. I have not reached, and I will never reach, a place from which I can coast into heaven. Father, I have sinned against heaven and before you. I am not worthy to be called your son.

Again, how seriously do we mean this? Does it make sense to go to confession if we don't? But dare we *not* go when a loving God begs us to be healed of all that is making us unhappy?

I Cannot Save Myself

The most dangerous heresy man falls into is that which says, "If I *try* hard enough, I can be holy." Or: "If I really wanted to stop sinning, I could." Both are hopeless positions — pulling myself up by the bootstraps, or trying to create the life of God by myself.

"Without me you can do nothing" is not a scare tactic from Christ to make us try harder. It is the Vine saying to the branches: please remain in me. If you cut yourself off, there is no source of life for you, and you have no way of re-attaching yourself by your own power."

So, the crucial decision: I am sinful. I cannot save myself from the slightest sin by my own power. There is a loving God who offers healing and health, love and communion.

How seriously do I want it? Can my confession

be an offhand, routine "favor" done to God, or is it the S.O.S. sign given by one who is otherwise desperate?

Conversion Is Letting My Life Go into the Hands of God

It is once and for all, but it is never over with all at once. Some people have dramatic single experiences of conversion: Paul on the road to Damascus, Augustine hearing the child telling him to pick up the book and read, Francis embracing the leper. Most of us go through a long and gradual process, partly because that's the way human beings grow, partly because that's the way human beings delay.

But for all of us, Augustines or ordinary Smiths, conversion is ongoing. Paul and Augustine and Francis did not absolutely begin their conversion at those peak moments, and their healing certainly did not stop with them. We may be out of the hospital, but we still need medicine. The fever is gone, but the virus still lurks. The broken bone or the torn ligament has healed, but it needs continuing exercise.

The call of the Spirit is absolute: The Lord gently presses for totally healed men and women, because he cannot love us with limits. Yet the Spirit is also patient with our fragile determination and human limitations.

On the one hand, then, some of us may still have to come to terms with God's call. We may never really have turned to God in an explicit, childlike act of self-dedication. We may never have turned away from the greater or lesser attitude of sinful self-preoccupation in our lives. Some of us may have done so, more or less wholeheartedly, and kept at it. If we are honest, we have no doubts as to what still needs to be done. And some, like the Mother Teresas of the world, have accepted the gift with all their heart — and then make the humblest confessions of all.

Many devout Catholics, no longer pressured one way or another into frequent confession, ask about what frequency there should be. It is a question almost impossible to answer. (Suppose someone said, "Every 17 days." Would it help?)

How often can I be very serious about this expression of real sinfulness, real and felt need of healing, confident expectation of divine help, willingness to make an authentic sign? How often do I need to admit my failures in purely human situations, i.e., to keep my spirit from becoming dulled and forgetful?

The question really is, how often can I seriously and profitably celebrate the *sacrament* of reconciliation, i.e., the sign, the community celebration, the individual external expression of sorrow and worship, the public statement that God alone heals? There are other ways of being forgiven: personal and fraternal prayer of faith, especially in the Eucharist.

One person says she sometimes "needs" to go twice in a week; another says four times a year is adequate for him. On the one hand, we have to avoid mere mindless repetition; on the other, we need to discipline ourselves even in the most sacred aspects of our life. We must take the responsibility upon ourselves.

Human Beings Can't Live
Without Making Signs

We have just touched on what may be the most difficult problem about confession. Why, indeed, should confession be *in words,* to a priest, within the community, externally? Why not keep it between me and God?

The problem is not solved by stating that it is essential to human nature to express interior feelings in external ways, or that whatever is inside must come out, or it's really not inside. If we have to be *forced,* by argument or law, the results are apt to be superficial. If I am really sorry I will give some sign to my friend; if I really love, I will show it. I will not do anything with relish that I don't really feel.

The answer lies in the nature of the church, i.e., the particular community to which I belong. The community may, unfortunately, be represented by only one priest. But *somebody* must be the sign of God's graciousness to me or I will shrink away from any self-revelation. There is no point in expressing sorrow or asking forgiveness if there is no reason to think someone is interested in me.

A. The Priest: The emphasis on community may seem to diminish the role of the priest. But every community needs someone to gather around. The priest is the center of unity. Just as the whole church is a visible sign of the love of Christ, so the priest is the visible center of unity. The whole church is the Body of Christ, the means whereby he is visible to the world today. The priest makes Christ visible as the Head of his Body.

Some priests have become embarrassed at what seems to be excessive deference given them by the laity. They want to be "like everybody else." Understandable though this is, it is a misreading of the *sacramental* role of the priest. He is not the leader because he is wiser or holier — though he may be. He is at the center because there needs to be a living, human, individual sign of the living individual Christ the Head.

Renewal of the sacrament of confession means that the priest must continue (or begin) to *reveal* the ever-present forgiveness of God. He makes visible the forgiveness of Jesus, not in a magical and merely ritualistic way, but by himself feeling and expressing the love of Christ. He must be able "to enter the heart of another without hobnail boots, but rather with the delicacy of a friend lifting a friend from where he has fallen among thorns." He must be sensitive, yet honest, helping the penitent to search his heart, admit his sinfulness and experience the love of God.

In *Philemon's Problem* Father James Burtchaell, C.S.C., has this to say about the confessor: "If a man is to reach into the hearts of another with the forceful candor and delicate gentleness of Jesus Christ, then it is a highly personal task, and calls for a man of sensitivity, honesty, savvy and compassion . . .

"Men of profound and singlehearted affection and service must speak out the simple call of Jesus and must ask for the companionship of everyone they pass, most particularly the most offensive or inert . . . .

"The priest reveals to the penitent that in the face

69

of his pettiness and fault, he loves him all the same, he loves him all the more. And so he embodies the love of the Father and of the Son, who cherish men in their deepest misery."

B. *The Community:* Except in emergencies, individual confession is required. But the new ritual will almost certainly "canonize" the communal celebration of the sacrament. It cannot be repeated too often that God's method of forgiving is through other people. We are reconciled to him by being reconciled with his Body.

Conversion makes us realize that God's gifts are not for our private satisfaction but for sharing with others. We cannot separate individual conversion from a commitment to a more fraternal, more peaceful family, neighborhood, Church, nation and world. We are not entrusted with freedom and grace in isolation from others, but as operating members of a Body. More than that, we need others as they need us.

We sin against others. God forgives us through them. In some way or other, I have hurt all these people in church with me. (Perhaps some standing there have more vivid memories of it than I do.) But even if those I have hurt the most are absent, this is the community of Christ which has suffered because of me. I join in the common plea for forgiveness.

But the community also has the duty of being the visible forgiveness of Christ to me. St. Francis loved priests because "we see nothing on this earth of the Body and Blood of Christ except in the Eucharist which they consecrate." That is true. But the

Eucharist is meant to produce another Christ — the community which makes visible his love. It is true to say that we see nothing of the love of Christ on earth today except in the love of human beings. And if that love is to be expected any place, it is in that group which has been privileged to become the Body of Christ.

The communal celebration of the sacrament of reconciliation is a rich sacramental action, therefore. It is a group of individuals forming a forgiving body in union with Christ. It is also a being-forgiven community, receiving the healing of Christ. Each individual forgives his brothers and sisters (representing all who are not there) and is forgiven by all his brothers and sisters. In the process God says, "Has no one else condemned you? Neither do I condemn you. Go in peace."

The Individual Confession

Two points may be helpful.

First, the individual confession made during a communal celebration will have to be much briefer than the more leisurely and thorough one made when there is only one penitent.

It may be helpful, then, to recall an old practice of concentrating on one's "predominant fault." It would be better to say, "one's predominant characteristic." Each of us is a composite of qualities, decisions, temperament, history, habit. Our five best friends, writing separately, would agree essentially if asked to describe our principal characteristics.

Now, it is precisely in our dominant charac-

71

teristics that our potential and our danger lie. Suppose someone is a leader ("Napoleon") type. He or she has the talent to organize, drive, cajole, repair, plan and complete almost any project you have in mind, whether it's running the K. of C. dance, the 82nd Airborne, the liturgical committee or the First National Bank. Faith, love, commitment to Christ will probably be expressed mostly in leadership, and that is as God intended. But this person has the vices of his or her virtues. By the same token, "bossiness," running roughshod over others, impatience, inconsiderateness, a domineering attitude, will be the area in which this person sins. Attila the Hun and Joan of Arc had the same characteristic.

Now, when this person confesses, what is the particular area that most needs healing (and to the end of his or her life, since the impulse will always be there)? Obviously the abuse of one's characteristic talent. Such a person might well say, "I am a very dominating person, and since my last confession I have caused others pain by not letting them have their say, forcing them to do what I wanted. I have been more concerned with getting things done than with how my wife or children felt. A few times I became so angry because my plans were balked that I hurt others' feelings with sarcasm and even unjust accusations."

There's a lifetime of gradual healing indicated there!

Another person's main asset-liability may be sensitiveness, quickness of perception, placidness, orderliness, imagination, expansiveness, reserve, depth. Each person is unique, hence each confession is by nature unique to that person.

The second thing to be said about individual confession has to do with *sign*. To celebrate a sacrament is to *make a sign,* and perhaps nothing will help us more to appreciate the need of the sacrament than a growing consciousness of the importance of signs in our life.

We need a *sign* from God that he forgives us. We *know* he does, yes. But it is only human to want to see and hear and feel it. God understands and gives us what we need. Confession is a *sign* Christ gives us, here and now. He is always present to us — he does not "come" to us in confession or Communion. Rather, he becomes *visible* (audible, touchable) because as human beings we need to see and hear and touch to be fully human. Every sacrament is an act of God, of Christ, of his Spirit, here and now, and we have visible and reassuring proof of it.

The sacrament is a sign the church makes to us that the community welcomes us, reconciles us. We receive the sign from the church, and we give it as members of the church. We are the visible love of Christ to each other and to the world.

The sacrament is a sign that we give to God, a sign that we trust him, believe in his love for us. It is a public, humble sign that we admit we are sinners. It is a sign that we have hope that evil can be destroyed and God's life can be lived. It is a sign that we are willing to be healed, to grow, to take our responsible place in the community.

Both in the individual confession and in the communal celebration, much will depend on the ability and willingness of both priest and penitent(s) to be expressive of the full meaning of the sacrament. We are not entirely comfortable with this as yet. It will take time to develop a greater realism about our sinfulness as well as a greater sense of the social nature of our sinfulness. We will be healed in the process of trying.

Eucharist

There was a grain of truth in the excessive scrupulosity of those who would never go to Communion without having gone to confession each time. All sacraments, are oriented toward the great sacrament and sacrifice of Christian unity. We are healed so that we may truly be the community of Christ, gathered around him to offer praise and thanks to the Father. The church is never so much the church as when it is the visibly united Body of Christ expressing the love that binds its members together and to the Lord, and being strengthened in that love.

The Eucharist itself is a healing and forgiving sacrament, not just in the penitential prayers said at the beginning, but in its whole meaning and purpose. The Eucharist is the saving death and resurrection of Jesus made present to us for our salvation. We are healed, forgiven, reconciled as the family of Christ and as individuals. There is no greater remedy for sin than the Body and blood of Christ which we take. There is no greater reconciliation than the union of Jesus and his community, and the members of the community with each other.

It is necessary that we have the sign of forgiveness in a sacrament in which we healthily concentrate on ourselves as sinners and on God as forgiving. After that, in the Eucharist, we give the full beautiful sign of what confession has begun — the community of Christ fulfilling its purpose, praising the Father through him and in his Spirit.

Chapter VI

An Imaginary Confession
According to the New Ritual

The following may help penitents become used to the new rite. All that the priest and penitent say (except for Scripture reading by the priest and the actual confession and counseling) is printed in boldface type, for easy use in private confession.

Imagining a confession is like writing love letters for sale to an unknown buyer: the result may be completely divorced from reality.

But the project seems worth the effort. All of us, priests and penitents (and priest-penitents!) are being called to find greater depth and meaning in our confession. The following attempt at filling out the directions of the new ritual may at least serve as something to criticize and improve on.

1. Preparation by Priest and Penitent. "Priest and penitent should first prepare themselves by prayer to celebrate the sacrament. The priest should call upon the Holy Spirit so that he may receive enlightenment and charity. The penitent should compare his life with the example and commandments of Christ and then pray to God for the forgiveness of sins."

This seems to indicate priest and penitent praying separately. But there is no reason why they cannot also pray together. For instance: *Priest:* Jesus, you are present with us here, to heal and strengthen. I pray that your kindness and mercy may show through me, so that this brother (or sister) of yours may truly meet you in this sacramental sign. May your Spirit fill both of us, so that we may face the truth of sin, but still more the saving truth of your all-powerful love.

This brother (sister) is very dear to you. May I do or say nothing that will keep him from your love. Help me to understand how he feels. Help me to love him as you do, this person for whom you died, and whom you want to heal and strengthen.

Help me to realize the importance of this action in me. Help me to be sensitive and sympathetic, but also frank and honest.

Above all help me to show this person the sign of your unlimited love.

Penitent: Dear Lord, I come to you as one who needs healing and forgiveness. I have been guilty of not responding to your call to friendship. I have allowed selfishness to spoil to some degree the good life you give me. I have not honored you as I should, and I have not given others the love that you called me to give them.

Help me now to face my true self honestly — all the good you have done in me, and all the evil —

whatever evil, big or small — that I knowingly or unknowingly have allowed to develop in my life.

I truly believe that you are here to heal me, to reconcile me to yourself and to my brothers and sisters in your Body, the church. I know that your love has never ceased. I thank you for bringing me to you. Give me strength now, for I do not want to face myself. I do not like to admit that I have done wrong.

Help me to see clearly what I must do to let you repair the damage I have done to myself and others and to your honor. Help me to appreciate again the gift of life you have given me.

(Possibly) Priest and penitent together:

Our Father, we believe in your love for us. Jesus, we believe in your healing presence. Spirit of love and truth, we trust in your power to recreate and reconcile, to cleanse and heal, to make life grow again, to fill us with the fire of your love.

We begin this sacrament with reverence. It is your action in ours. We pray that we may sincerely and seriously listen for your word and your will. We want this holy sacrament to be a pure and truthful act of worship of you. We place ourselves entirely in your hands. We want to be open to whatever you will.

2. Receiving the Penitent. Obviously, if priest and penitent have prayed together, the welcome will already have been given. The priest, in any case, is reminded to receive the penitent kindly and to speak to him pleasantly.

The penitent, and, fittingly, the priest, signs himself with the sign of the cross and says:

Penitent: **In the name of the Father and of the Son and of the Holy Spirit. Amen.**

The priest encourages the penitent to have confidence in God. He may use his own words or any of several formal expressions suggested in the ritual. One example:

Priest: **May God, who has enlightened every heart, help you to know your sins and trust in his mercy.**

Penitent: **Amen.**

3. *Reading the Word of God.* Then the priest, or the penitent himself, may read a text of holy Scripture, or this may be done as part of the preparation for the sacrament. Through the word of God the Christian receives light to recognize his sins and is called to conversion and to confidence in God's mercy.

Choice can be made of numerous texts; actually one can choose anything appropriate from Scripture. The following passages are among those suggested from the New Testament:

Matthew 6, 14-15	John 20, 19-23
Luke 15, 1-7	Colossians 1, 12-14
Ephesians 5, 1-2	Luke 6, 31-38
I John 1, 6-7. 9	Romans 5, 8-9
Mark 1, 14-15	Colossians 3, 8-10. 12-17

The ritual says nothing about a period of silence after this reading, but such a pause (if circumstances permit) would no doubt deepen the reverence of both priest and penitent for what they are doing.

4. Confession of Sins and Acceptance of Penance. The penitent may begin with whatever formula is customary. Most people will probably continue what they have been doing all their lives.

The following is an IMAGINARY example of confession and the help a priest might give.

Penitent: "Father, I confess that I have been guilty of being a self-centered husband and father. I enjoy my work, but I spend too much time on it. I want to do nothing but work, work, work, not only to make money but because I like to use my hands. I know very well that my wife needs more, well, love from me, and I should spend more time with my children. I haven't paid much attention to what my wife says or to her feelings. I have been too tough and gruff and unfeeling. I want to do better, and I will try. That's about my worst sin, Father."

Priest: I'm sure God loves you for your willingness to admit your sin and for seeking his forgiveness. You want to do better. Now, can you think of some actual things you might do to make it better at home?

Penitent: Well, I ought to think about some of the things my wife needs. She works very hard, and she likes to go out once in a while. But I seldom ever take her out. I'm always "going" to take her to a nice restaurant some evening, but I never do. I'll try to do that next week, just the two of us.

81

Priest: What will be the best thing you can do for her when you take her out?

Penitent: Well, I guess . . . . I really just ought to pay attention to her. I guess I should talk to her more — well, and listen to what she's really saying — instead of just sitting there like a bump on a log.

Priest: What do you think she wants most?

Penitent: Gee, I don't know. She says she just wants to be with me, and that's hard for me to believe. I guess . . . maybe sometimes I don't feel I'm worth it. I want to get *busy* . . .

Priest: You sometimes feel you're not as good as she thinks you are, and you don't like to talk about it.

Penitent: Yes, I guess that's about it.

Priest: Do you love her?

Penitent: O sure! She's the greatest gal in the world! It's just that I . . .

Priest: But you think you're *not* the greatest guy in the world.

Penitent: Right!

Priest: Do you feel you have to cover up, by being tough, and busy, like John Wayne?

Penitent: Yes, some.

Priest: Do you think she would love you less if she really knew you?

Penitent: No. I'd have to say I'm sure she really wouldn't.

Priest: So you know that you really could take a chance in telling her how you feel, how you really love her, what your real worries are.

Penitent: Yes, that's right. I don't know why I don't do it. It's easy for me to talk about sports and things, but it's hard putting my feelings into words.

Priest: Do you think it might be a good penance for you to really get ready for that dinner out with your wife next week? No big deal. Maybe plan to take a ride afterwards, and really listen to her, and then, as naturally as you can, to try to tell her a little of how you feel?

Penitent: I guess I could give it a try.

Priest: Fine. And as part of this trying, how about praying a few minutes each day over this problem?

Penitent: O.K., I'll try.

Another imaginary example, worked out by Father John Berkemeyer, campus minister at the University of Cincinnati:

Penitent: "Father, I still have this problem with my parents, you know? I just can't seem to get along with them. Mom's on my back all the time and I'm always mad at her, then my father jumps on me for being mad at Mom. It's just a big hassle."

Priest: "I know what you mean, Pete. It seems hopeless at times. I don't think I really talked to my parents for several years. I always felt as if I could never do anything right."

Penitent: "What'd you do, Father? I know I have to do something. It's not that I hate them, but what I feel for them just isn't right."

Priest: "Well, you're on the right track. You know your feelings aren't what they should be and that's a good sign. Can you talk to your father at all?"

Penitent: "I think so — at least more than to Mom."

Priest: "Why don't you try it. Maybe figure out sometime when you two can be alone. Then try a little reverse psychology. Start out by telling him that you want to try to work things out. Let's make that your penance this time, all right?"

Penitent: "I'll give it a try. And if it doesn't work . . .

Priest: "If that doesn't work, Peter, well we'll just try something else next time."

Priest: You have honestly admitted your sinfulness to God. Now he gives you a new start. You die a little bit — or maybe a lot — as Jesus died on the cross. But you are given something too — you "rise" like Christ. He gives you this sign of his presence with you, his healing and forgiveness, his strength to make your life better. If you deepen your love for your wife, you will do better with your children — and this will help you with everyone else. If we are bad with one person, we are in danger of hurting everyone by the same attitude. So this sacrament is a way of helping you to be kind to everyone. By letting your wife love you, you will let God, and others, love you more, and you will have a better idea of why Jesus calls us together in his church, to help each other and to have peace with each other.

5. Penitent's Prayer Expressing Contrition for Sin ("Act of Contrition"). The priest will indicate to the penitent that he should now manifest (express) his sorrow for sin (already present in the preparation for the sacrament). The penitent may do this in the following (or similar) words:

My God,
I am sorry for my sins with all my heart.
In choosing to do wrong
and failing to do good,

I have sinned against you
whom I should love above all things.
I firmly intend, with your help,
to do penance,
to sin no more,
and to avoid whatever leads me to sin.
Our Savior Jesus Christ
suffered and died for us.
In his name, my God, have mercy.

This imaginary example is perhaps too idealistic in its quick "success." As the ritual says, the priest's help may be necessary to help the penitent make a complete confession. [Nothing new here: one must confess all (and only) mortal sinfulness.] Some penitents may need help in seeing the evil of their sins and in being truly sorry. Some may need to have their responsibilities pointed out to them — duties as Christian, husband or wife, father or mother, son or daughter, business, worker. A penitent may not realize that he has an obligation to repair material or spiritual damage done to others.

The penance, the ritual says, has reference not only to past sins but is to be a help towards a new life, a remedy for weakness. It should correspond to the nature of the sins confessed and their seriousness, insofar as possible. The penance is best done by prayer, self-denial, service of one's neighbor and works of mercy whereby the *social aspect of sin and its forgiveness* is made clear.

6. Sacramental Absolution. The priest now extends his hands (or at least his right hand) over the head of the penitent.

The (partly new) formula of sacramental absolution has great depth of meaning: 1) the reconciliation of the penitent has its source in the mercy of the Father; 2) it shows the connection between the reconciliation of the sinner and the death and resurrection of Christ; 3) the work of the Holy Spirit in the forgiveness of sins is seen; 4) the place of the church in the sacrament is evident from the fact that reconciliation with God is both sought and given through the ministry of the church.

7. *Proclaiming the Praise of God. Dismissal of Penitent.* The celebration quickly ends. After the absolution, the priest says:

Priest: **Give thanks to the Lord, for he is good.**
Penitent: **His mercy endures for ever.**

Then the priest dismisses the reconciled penitent with these words:

Priest: **The Lord has freed you from your sins. Go in peace.**

The ritual concludes: The penitent continues and expresses his conversion by a life which is re-formed according to the Gospel of Christ and more and more permeated by the love of God, for "charity covers a multitude of sins."

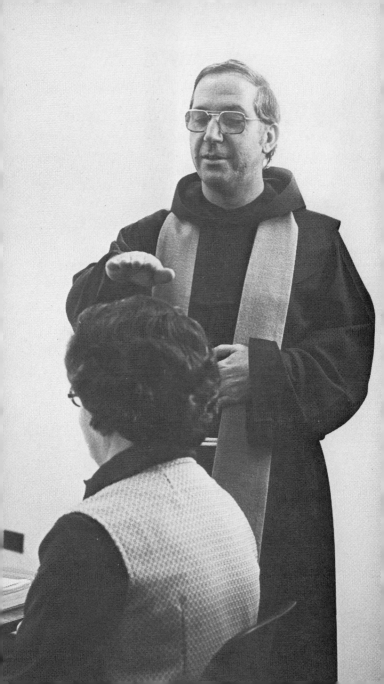

Appendix

How the Practice of Confession Changed Over the Centuries

In a time of change, it is good to recall the things that never change. The bedrock of Catholic faith is that *Jesus is Savior,* i.e., he makes visible and effective the merciful forgiveness of God. He and he alone saves us from sin. By his death and resurrection he can — and wills to — send his Spirit into the heart of any human being, releasing him from moral sickness and death and making him a living member of his family-community-body, the church.

Christ forgives those who sin, even seriously, after their baptismal conversion. He has made his community, the church, the sign and instrument of his forgiveness. "Whose sins you forgive, they are forgiven." Reconciliation with Christ's community is reconciliation with him.

It should be unnecessary to say that sincere admission of sin, sorrow and grace-full determination to avoid sin and live a life in Christ, are essentials of the ongoing conversion that must characterize

Christian life; and that a healing of the damage of past sins, as well as a continual "keeping in condition" for the future — whether this be called self-denial, mortification or "doing penance" — is an obvious element of authentic Catholic attitude and practice.

The substance is one thing; the manner of expressing it is another. It is important, even necessary in these days of change, for Catholics to realize that *a variety of practice* is nothing new in the church's history, especially in the sacrament of penance. The following thumbnail sketch is meant to do two things: 1) to reassure worried Catholics that the church is not off on some wild excursion of experiment; 2) to challenge all of us to continue the church's long search for the most fitting and effective way to *practice* its ministry of reconciliation.

The following pages are heavily indebted (i.e., the present author copied a lot) to Father Lawrence Landini, O.F.M., professor of history and liturgy at St. Leonard College, Dayton, Ohio; and to Dr. William Storey, professor of liturgy at the University of Notre Dame. Neither, of course, is responsible for the following material.

Holy Church, Sinful Members

The purpose of the church is to proclaim the forgiveness of God in Jesus. The forgiveness is absolute, free, totally loving, inexhaustible. Our Father is the "Prodigal Father" who runs to embrace us. "Even if your sins be as scarlet —".

For the first Christians, the church was an explosion of grace. Baptismal faith and love meant an entirely new creation. It was not merely the turning over of a new leaf, but a new life, filled by God's own Spirit.

Ideally, it was unthinkable that anyone who experienced this total change of life should throw away this treasure, reject God's friendship, return, as our Lord said, like a dog to his vomit. St. John says, "No one begotten of God acts sinfully, because he remains of God's stock; he cannot sin because he is begotten of God" (I Jn. 3, 9). *Hebrews* is even stronger: "When men have once been enlightened and have tasted the heavenly gift and become sharers in the Holy Spirit . . . and then have fallen away, it is impossible to make them repent again, since they are crucifying the Son of God for themselves and holding him up to contempt" (Hebrews 6, 4-6).

Yet the same New Testament records serious abuses in the young church. Corinth, for instance, does not present the picture of an ideal parish — a case of incest, factionalism, pride, even misconduct in connection with the Eucharist. And St. John speaks of those who have "turned aside from your early love" (Rev. 2, 4).

What was the Church to do with sinfulness *within* itself? Its primary purpose was to proclaim forgiveness to pagans. "Repent and be baptized, for the forgiveness of your sins." The forgiveness spoken of was primarily that of baptism, which supposed a total commitment to Christ in which defection was unthinkable.

The New Testament, then, shows a church that

didn't quite know, at first, what to do with the problem.

Paul had some stern words about the man who married his mother-in-law at Corinth: "I hand him over to Satan for the destruction of his flesh, so that his spirit may be saved on the day of the Lord" (I Cor. 5, 1-13).

About immoral persons he repeats the familiar phrase of the Old Testament: "Expel the wicked man from your midst."

To the Thessalonians Paul writes, "If anyone will not obey our injunction, delivered through this letter, single him out to be ostracized that he may be ashamed of his conduct. But do not treat him like an enemy; rather, correct him as you would a brother" (II Thess. 3, 14).

Thus, while the church has the power to *loose* a man from his sins, it also has the power to *bind* him in exclusion from the worshiping community.

It should be emphasized that the Eucharist was always seen as effecting the forgiveness of "daily," i.e., the real but not-spiritually-fatal, sinfulness. The *kiss of peace* was a sign of reconciliation and unity, and the receiving of communion ratified the new expression of brotherly and sisterly love in Christ.

But it took a long time for the church to work out a way of dealing with serious sin within itself. Until it did, sinners were left to the mercy of God. When "sinners" were prayed for in the early church, the reference was to these people.

Yet the church could not but realize that forgiveness was available for baptized Christians. The earliest ecclesiastical references to penance are con-

92

cerned for the salvation of all. There is fraternal correction, prayer, and, as has been indicated, exclusion from worship.

In the *Didache* and *I and II Clement* great importance is attached to confession of sins to God. "Confession" here is the same as doing penance. Insofar as this is manifested externally, confession before God becomes confession before men. "In the assembly confess your sins and go not to prayer (i.e., Eucharist) with an evil conscience!" But public accusation before God was couched in general form, (as in our *Confiteor*) without mention of particular sins. Detailed confession of sin lies altogether beyond the horizon of early Christian penitential procedure.

It is difficult to know whether the sinfulness referred to in these practices was mortal sinfulness or "daily" sin. At some point the church did deal with the former. Even without official intervention, one who had sinned seriously had to "judge" himself and separate himself from the communal celebration of the Eucharist. At the very least, his absence from Communion would give authorities the occasion to admonish him.

A famous prophet in Rome (140 A.D.) named Hermas (probably a brother of the Bishop of Rome) has left us a book (The *Shepherd*) which works out a doctrine whereby mortal sinners could be reconciled to the church, presupposing the doing of penance. *But only once in a lifetime.* (He believed the Second Coming of Christ to be imminent.)

It is evident from this document that what was implicit from the beginning had become a practice: a sinner who does penance is to be received back into the church. Even in Hermas the impossibility of a second forgiveness rests on psychological and moral, not dogmatic, grounds.

This was a great step (or the record of a great step) for the church. Just as it had prayed "I believe in *one* baptism" so it prayed that it believed "in *one* penance."

At the close of the apostolic period, the church more or less clearly lived according to these principles: 1) Every sin calls for penance; 2) no sin, even the gravest, is excluded from forgiveness, provided there is real conversion and penance; 3) prayer and works of mercy are means of obtaining the forgiveness of sins; one's personal prayer receives effective support from the prayer of the faithful; 4) confession of sins is sometimes joined to prayer; 5) rulers of the Christian community are obliged to admonish the guilty and even to excommunicate them to bring about final reconciliation; 6) reconciliation with the body of believers is a guarantee of forgiveness by God.

In the third century, the Montanist movement protested what it felt was a growing laxity in the church. It held that the church *could* forgive sins, but it must not do so, lest others sin. The movement reached its peak in Africa, under Tertullian.

Orders of Penitents

In the course of time there were two developments: 1) Those who committed serious sin would enter an "order" of penance — which became a real

94

class of members of the church — and wait for their one-time deathbed reconciliation. Only a tiny handful, it seems, received Communion. There were "Communion Masses" and "non-Communion" Masses. (Older Catholics who remember the 11:00 or 12:00 o'clock Masses on Sunday morning 30 or 40 years ago will realize that this was not an exclusive characteristic of the early church.) So, for a thousand years, Catholics received the Eucharist rarely, because reconciliation was so difficult. For most people there were only two Communions — their first, and *Viaticum.*

So, just as the church elaborated a catechumenate of preparation for baptism for two to four years (a practice which the church wishes to reinstate), so it also worked out a "second catechumenate" for readmission to the church after serious sin. Reconciliation was no "quickie" affair. It involved a series of stages lasting for years. The penitent had to be "re-sponsored" as he was the first time; he had to be re-instructed in the Christian life. The first "confessors" were co-sponsors who would fast and pray with the penitent for the long period of his second catechumenate.

Above all, forgiveness was something to be *prayed for,* not simply taken as automatic. The prayers of the penitent, of his sponsor and of the church were seen as very important.

Several orders of penitents came into existence. First, there were the "Weepers" who stood (or prostrated themselves outside the church door; second, the "Kneelers" who could kneel at the back of church inside the door. Kneeling was a sign of being a sinner. Everyone else had to stand for Mass; third, those who were allowed to *stand*. Finally, at Easter or Holy Thursday, there was the grand reconciliation; the penitents were welcomed back to full communion with the church, by the laying on of hands by the bishop (this practice, a sign of union remains in the priest's extending his hands (or hand) over the head of the penitent while giving absolution). The reconciliation was dramatic and public, and approved by the congregation.

The public sins for which public penance was required were the notorious triad of apostasy, adultery and murder. In some cases the sin was thought so heinous that forgiveness was given only on one's deathbed. In the meantime, the sinner had to fast, and abstain from marital relations.

It was the whole penitential discipline, not just this final liturgical act, which was considered as bringing about forgiveness and the grace of the Spirit.

A second development was the re-thinking of the whole matter of reconciliation. Already in the fourth century the church came to the conclusion that the sacrament of penance, or reconciliation, could be repeated. It *could* be. But the first bishops to initiate the practice were reproved or removed from office. St. John Chrysostom, patriarch of Constantinople, was one of the first bishops in the church to absolve repeatedly. It was a "scandal" and contributed to his downfall.

The break with severity began in the third century, for three reasons: 1) the Arian heresy, which denied that Christ was God; 2) the Donatist heresy, which among other things held that a sacrament is invalid if administered by an unworthy priest; 3) the persecution of Diocletian. The mass of these "unreliable" Christians who fell away found the penitential discipline of the Church too severe. Hence, they preferred to avoid the discipline by putting off reconciliation for a long time.

Thus, there was little recourse to the sacrament, and public penance began to lose its effectiveness, though it remained solemn and severe. There was an increase in the specified kinds of grave sins which needed to be atoned for and forgiven within the penitential discipline. Even after reconciliation, there were lingering penalties which the forgiven sinner had to observe for the rest of his life.

Only those of mature years were admitted to the Order of Penitents, since Penance was given only once. There was much writing in this period against the rigorism of the Novatian heresy, which denied the church's power to absolve heretics, idolaters, murderers, adulterers, and fornicators. There was an attempt to discern the role of the church in God's giving of forgiveness. By reconciliation with the church, the sinner was able to return to God.

Gradually, some kind of principle had to be adopted for reconciliation — one that would balance severity and practical pastoral needs. Men like St. Cyprian inclined toward greater and greater leniency. There was complaint about over-hasty concession of forgiveness. Actually, neither St. Cyprian nor Pope Cornelius, who also was willing to forgive the persecution-apostates easily, did anything new. They speeded up the period of penance necessary before reconciliation with the church.

The doing of penance, whatever the changes in actual practice of reconciliation, was a major element in the sacrament. The sacrament was a "laborious baptism," and the severity of the penance, sometimes lifelong, was a far cry from our relatively easy practice.

The Beginning of Private Confession

There is apparent a growing pressure against public penance: 1) as the emphasis on interiority grew; 2) as the rigor of penitential discipline became harder to bear — the satisfaction required was severe, sometimes lasting for life; 3) as the practice of "waiting till the end" continued. At least one Bishop, Caesar of Arles, encouraged his people to prepare for this penance before death even though they were not able to participate in the public canonical penance of the church. Father Cyrille Vogel, a historian of dogma, concludes: "It is extremely probable that the faithful who, at the exhortation of their pastors, sincerely repented and tried by good works to merit penance at death, were admitted without reconciliation to the Eucharistic table."

So-called auricular (i.e., "to the ear") confession came into the church by the back door. The stance of public reconciliation was maintained rigidly — but there was a pastoral problem of how to deal with ordinary sinners. The solution came through monasticism. Sometime toward the end of the sixth century, and in the seventh, a new mode of the church's ministry of forgiving sins appeared on the continent. It seems that the new trend originated in the Celtic churches of Ireland and England.

From the earliest days the monks had a practice of "revelation of conscience." They were asked to go to a "spiritual father" (not necessarily a priest) to whom they could tell their current spiritual condition, their problems, temptations, etc.

The practice became widespread both among monks and lay people. The confessor might fast or pray with the penitent for several days, and then assure him in the name of God, the Gospel, and the community that he was indeed forgiven.

It would seem that this was not, strictly speaking, absolution in the modern sense. Rather, it was assurance coming from someone of great faith, basing his words on the Gospel: "I tell you the Gospel: you are forgiven."

Confessors would give appropriate advice and were accustomed to measuring out penalties in proportion to the guilt confessed. It is now that we have the "Penitential Books" with "tariffed" (i.e., specified) penances. These books indicated specifically what particular penance was called for by a particular sin.

Thus there grew up a practice greatly divergent from that of the early church: In the ancient canonical discipline, 1) only certain grave public sins were confessed; 2) this was done to the bishop; 3) there was a time of satisfaction *before* reconciliation with the church; 4) there was a reconciliation ceremony.

In the new mode of penitential discipline which developed, 1) all sinners approached as often as they

99

wished; 2) penitents addressed themselves ordinarily in secret to a priest, not a bishop; 3) the
priest identified the penance for each sin according
to the specifications of a penitential book;
4) penitents then left and performed their penance;
5) they returned for final absolution.

Some of the penances prescribed by the penitential books were fastings, vigils, bodily mortification,
praying the psalms, giving alms, abstinence from
sexual intercourse, and pilgrimages.

Sometimes these penances were so severe that
they could not possibly be done in one lifetime (like
consecutive prison terms today). The result was a
system of substitutions or commutations. One could
substitute saying the 150 psalms three times for a
year of fasting, etc. One could also find a holy person to do penance for one's sins. It takes no great
amount of imagination to picture the abuses that
resulted from this practice.

In the ninth century, as part of the reform under
Alcuin, there was stress on confession to a priest and
the intervention of the church and interior forgiveness. Attempts were made to outlaw the penitential
handbooks and to revive public penance. But any
results of the attempt to bring order into chaotic
practice collapsed with the crumbling of the
Carolingian empire. Public and private penance
overlapped. Since there were many kinds of "penance," there arose a tendency to laxity through the
choice of the least burdensome.

There seems to have been a new principle in-
voked: private penance for private sins, public penance for public sins. This was new in the sense that

formerly all serious sins fell under one canonical penitential discipline.

Around the year 1000, absolution of sins (the term itself was new — formerly the word was "re-conciliation") was given immediately after confession of sins before the penance was carried out.

To sum up, by the 12-13th century, there were three modalities of penance: 1) Solemn Public Penance was imposed for particularly scandalous sins. These were reserved (i.e., for forgiveness) to the bishop and penance was under his supervision. It resembled the ancient canonical discipline. Sinners entered on Ash Wednesday, were reconciled on Holy Thursday. This solemn Public Penance could not be repeated.

2) Non-Solemn Public Penance was for less scandalous sins and could be imposed by pastors. For the most part it consisted of a simple ceremony at the church door (the pilgrim's door) in which the penance of making a pilgrimage was imposed. Pardon was granted upon return, or was given at the place of pilgrimage by "pardoners" located there.

3) Private sacramental confession came from the practice of the Celtic monks described above. This form of penance was open for everyone, for all sins, and could be repeated.

Theology of penance began to be developed in the 12th century. All 12th-century theologians were "contritionists," i.e., they gave preponderance to interior contrition. But the question inevitably arose: why confess, if sins are already forgiven by contrition? The first answer given was: to enable the priest to make a sound judgment. The question also arose:

Is the confession of sins a divine or ecclesiastical law?

Some theologians said absolution had only "declarative" value — contrition had already forgiven sins. Satisfaction, once greatly emphasized, was seen to be accessory, since it could be done after absolution.

The famous law of 1215, *Omnis utriusque sexus* ("All, of both sexes," i.e., must receive the sacrament) marked a definite step in the history of the sacrament. For grave sin confession was now required once a year, and to one's own pastor. There was far greater emphasis on the importance of the absolution itself. Theologians denied the sacramental nature of the former practice of confession to laymen.

In very brief form, the doctrine of Thomas Aquinas is as follows: The entire sacrament is the sign and the cause of the justification of the sinner. God's grace begets love in the sinner; he rises from slavish to filial fear. Contrition, perfected by love, wipes out sin. But sacramental confession is still necessary: the virtue of penance and the absolution together form the sacrament.

The Council of Trent

Luther held that the sinner is radically corrupt; he is incapable of repenting. He is aware of this, and is terrified; he abandons himself with confidence to God, who then "imputes" the merits of Christ to the sinner. God then looks on the sinner *as if* he were justified. The disposition of the sinner is one of faith and trust, and this alone forgives. The priest is simply the proclaimer of the Good News when he absolves the sinner. Christ, said Luther, did not intend confession as a sacrament, for it was not possible that out of a corrupt heart, there could come contrition that would obtain the forgiveness of sins: this would do an injustice to the all-encompassing merit of Christ.

The Council of Trent in 1551 taught: 1) Penance is truly and properly a sacrament. 2) The absolution is not merely "declarative." 3) There is a distinction between perfect and imperfect contrition. Perfect contrition is that which is made perfect by love of God. It includes the desire to receive the sacrament. Such sorrow effects reconciliation before the actual receiving of the sacrament. Imperfect contrition is that which is motivated by the seriousness, number and disgracefulness of sin, the loss of eternal happiness, and the incurring of eternal damnation. It cannot "justify" (i.e., bring one into the state of grace, because it does not, by definition, include the love of God described in perfect contrition), yet it disposes a man to receive the grace of God in the sacrament. 4) All mortal sins must be confessed, along with circumstances that change the nature of the sin. 5) Confession is necessary for those who commit mortal sin and is of divine institution. The secret manner of confessing is not foreign to the institution and command of Christ. 6) Bishops and priests only are the bearers of the power of the keys. 7) Since there are remnants of sin (temporal punishment) remaining after the sacrament, priests have a serious obligation to impose a penance.

The Roman ritual of 1614 prescribed that the priest, in surplice and stole, should receive confessions in the church and in a confessional. Abuses, for which confessors were both justly and unjustly accused, brought the requirement of the grate (screen) in the confessional. The bringing of the sacrament into the church and the privacy of the confessional gave a new solemnity to the sacrament and emphasized, at least implicitly, the respect of worship.

Since the Council of Trent, there has been little development, dogmatically or liturgically, in the sacrament of Penance.

But one great medieval and post-Reformation development was not only to insist that Catholics *use* the sacrament, but that it become a way of revealing oneself to the priest, explaining oneself, in order to be counseled. Thus a great system of pastoral counseling arose, which is one of the most important facets of the post-Reformation church. Confession was not to be a "quickie" matter.

The fact that it did become such — and has collapsed — may be due to the fact that instead of small parishes of 200-300 people, each of whom a priest might know, most parishes grew into the thousands.

In the post-Reformation church what was important was not an actual reconciliation with a congregation of people, nor even the long customary serious doing of penance, but a personal (and sometimes mechanical) confrontation with a priest, usually anonymously. There was little sense of being reconciled with the church. "Absolution" became the most important thing.

Today the church is groping toward further growth. What really is sin? What is the most effective way the church can celebrate the sacrament? How can we come to a deeper sense of the alienation sin produces in us — from God and community? Do we feel any real need for reconciliation with that community as such, and of course with those we hurt more directly by our sinfulness?

One style of celebrating the sacrament has all but collapsed. But the sacrament will never be lost. Throughout the centuries, the church has worked its way through various stages, usually with great difficulty, but always under the guidance of the Spirit. We will continue this painful growth now, in the new world we live in. The manner will be new, the substances will remain the same. The new ritual, *with proper preparation,* can be a gracious instrument of the Spirit.